Presented to:

Mamie Ruth Crawford
Henderson Middle School
770-504-2310 Ext: 146

Date:

VOICES OF HOPE

TIMELESS EXPRESSIONS OF FAITH FROM AFRICAN AMERICANS

HONOR HB BOOKS

Inspiration and Motivation for the Seasons of Life

An Imprint of Cook Communications Ministries • Colorado Springs, CO

Unless otherwise noted, all Scripture quotations are taken from the *King James Version* of the Bible.

09 08 07 06 05   10 9 8 7 6 5 4 3 2 1

Voices of Hope—Timeless Expressions of Faith from African Americans
ISBN 1-56292-342-0

Copyright © 2005 Bordon Books
6532 E. 71st Street, Suite 105
Tulsa, OK 74133

Published by Honor Books,
An Imprint of Cook Communications Ministries
4050 Lee Vance View
Colorado Springs, CO 80918

Manuscript compiled by Niral R. Burnett
Cover designed by Koechel Peterson and Associates

TABLE OF CONTENTS

Introduction 7

Biographical Sketches 9

Courage 31

Faith and Hope 39

Unity 61

Comfort 65

Strength 78

Wisdom 94

Forgiveness 102

Perseverance 104

Our Need for Christ 123

Thanksgiving 145

Integrity 159

Freedom and Future Glory 170

Endnotes 188

Success is to be measured not so much by the position that one has reached in life as by the obstacles which he has overcome while trying to succeed.

—BOOKER T. WASHINGTON

INTRODUCTION

It is an acknowledged truth that words have the power to change our lives. As you flip through the pages of *Voices of Hope*, you will find eternal truths that have been written and spoken by well-known African Americans through the years and collected for today's reader.

You will be moved by the powerful quotations, poems, speeches, songs, and excerpts on such topics as perseverance, freedom, integrity, courage, and faith. These words of truth by famous African Americans will instill hope in your soul, encourage you to keep the faith, and motivate you to transform your life into one that makes a difference for God in your world.

BIOGRAPHICAL SKETCHES

JOHN QUINCY ADAMS

John Quincy Adams was born in Frederick County, Virginia in 1845. His escape from slavery gave him the inspiration to write from personal experience a narrative that strongly revealed the evils of slavery. He published it in 1872.

RICHARD ALLEN

Born a slave, Richard Allen was able to purchase his freedom and continued his life in hard labor. Eventually, God called him to be a preacher of the Gospel, and he soon became the founder of the African Methodist Episcopal Church, which still thrives to this day.

THOMAS ANDERSON

Thomas Anderson was born a slave under the worst conditions, as he had a slave-master that was especially cruel. Yet through all of his persecutions, he had an experience with God that caused him to give his heart to Jesus and never look back. Anderson is the author of the *Interesting Account of Thomas Anderson, A Slave, Taken From His Lips*, which is a narrative of his conversion.

MAYA ANGELOU

World famous poet, actor, and historian Maya Angelou was born Marguerite Johnson in 1928, in St. Louis, Missouri. Angleou was raised in Arkansas where she was exposed to the evils of racism and segregation. Angelou became one of the first African-American women to produce a best-seller with her book, *I Know Why the Caged Bird Sings*. She was also very active in the Civil Rights Movement and, at the request of Martin Luther King Jr., Angelou became the northern coordinator for the Southern Leadership Conference. She has made hundreds of appearances on television and has taught on numerous college campuses, making guest appearances and also working as a professor.

WELLINGTON BOONE

Bishop Wellington Boone is the founder and bishop of The Father's House in Atlanta, Georgia. He has given his life to challenging people to develop godly character and is a crusader for reconciliation across racial and denominational lines. He is the founder of the Back to the Bible Movement and is a frequent speaker with Promise Keepers. He is the founder and chief prelate of the Fellowship of International Churches and founder of Global Outreach Campus Ministries, The Making of Champions, and the Boone Institute for Leadership Development.

VIRGINIA W. BROUGHTON

Virginia Broughton was a missionary who was born in Virginia to slaves. She was an advocate of women's rights and used the Scriptures to further her cause. This method of advocacy flew in the face of many in the nineteenth century. Broughton is the author of *Women's Work, as Gleaned from the Women of the Bible*. She also wrote a book entitled *Twenty Years' Experience as a Missionary*.

HENRY "BOX" BROWN

Henry "box" Brown was a slave who, after losing his family to the slave trade, found himself obsessed with the idea of escaping to freedom in the North. After praying, the idea occurred to him that he should ship himself in a courier box to a free state. Convinced that God had given him this inspiration, he proceeded to enlist the help of a carpenter and fashioned a box three feet, one inch wide and two feet, six inches high. Henry entered the box on the 29th day of March 1849 and had a friend ship him from Richmond. After twenty-seven hours inside, Henry arrived safely in the home of friends in Philadelphia.

LES BROWN

Although he received no formal education past high school, Les Brown has risen to become one of the most prominent motivational speakers in the country. Brown has grown to be one of the greatest thinkers and observers of human behavior of our time. He focuses on human potential in order to catapult listeners into new levels of achievement. He has also succeeded as a community leader, political commentator, and three-term congressman. He is the founder of Les Brown Unlimited and a best-selling author.

JOHN HENRIK CLARKE

Born in 1915 in Union Springs, Alabama, John Henrik Clarke was a writer, educator, and historian. As a champion of African-American causes, he helped introduce African-American studies to schools across the United States. While teaching in numerous universities, Clarke pioneered the idea that Black history should be studied by all citizens of the world.

ANDRAE CROUCH

There may be no other gospel artist in history who has had the impact of Andrae Crouch. Artists such as Elvis Presley, Paul Simon, and many gospel artists have sung his music for more than forty years. Beginning with his first band, The Church of God in Christ Singers, Crouch showed an unusual gift for music. In 1965, Crouch formed his first major group, the Disciples, and appeared often in both religious and secular venues, always proclaiming the Good News and saving power of Jesus through his music. Later in his career, he produced songs for well-known musicians such as Michael Jackson, Quincy Jones, and Diana Ross. Crouch is the current pastor of New Christ Memorial Church of God in Christ, which was founded by his parents.

GAIL DEVERS

After winning the gold metal in the 100-meter dash at the 1987 Pan-American Games and becoming the UCLA champion in 1988, Devers was on top of the world as an athlete. Then tragedy struck when sickness took hold of her body and nearly derailed her career. Instead of succumbing to sickness, Devers chose to move forward in her career as an athlete. In the course of her life she has won numerous Olympic medals and athletic honors and is only the third American athlete to be chosen for five Olympic track teams.

FREDERICK DOUGLASS

Frederick Douglass is arguably one of the greatest voices for human rights in American history. From his humble beginnings as a slave, Douglass advanced to abolitionist, publisher, and advisor to President Lincoln. He also served as the United States Ambassador to Haiti. Further, he was a minister of the gospel and lived his life in service to God with compassion toward His people.

W. E. B. DUBOIS

W. E. B. DuBois was born in 1868 in Great Barrington, Massachusetts. He is the founder of the National Association for the Advancement of Colored People. He graduated from Fisk University and afterwards earned a bachelor's degree from Harvard University. DuBois went on to earn his master's and doctorate degrees from Harvard. He is the author of the book, *The Souls of Black Folks,* and was the editor of the periodical, *The Crisis.*

ELIZABETH

Old Elizabeth received her calling to be an evangelist at only twelve years old. She did not preach much until she was forty-two years old. As a woman, she was rejected by many church leaders, but by God's ability, was able to travel and hold great meetings in the United States and Canada. She continued preaching into her ninety-seventh year.

ANTHONY EVANS SR.

Anthony Evans Sr. is the founder and pastor of the Oak Cliff Fellowship Church in Dallas, Texas. He founded Urban Alternative, an organization built to bring spiritual renewal to inner-city America. He was also a chaplain of the Dallas Cowboys football team for a time. Evans is currently a professor of theology at Dallas Theological Seminary and chaplain of the Dallas Mavericks basketball team.

JULIA A. J. FOOTE

A daughter of former slaves, Foote was born in 1823. She embraced Christianity at an early age and joined the African Methodist Episcopal church at fifteen years old. She later got married and began sensing a call to preach. However, her calling was met with much resistance because she was a woman. As an evangelist, Foote became the first female deacon of the AME church in 1894. She also became the second ordained female elder just before her death in 1900.

GEORGE FOREMAN

Former world heavyweight champion George Foreman has become a household name, associated with his boxing career as well as his business enterprises, which markets, among other things, the hugely-popular George Foreman grill. In addition, Foreman is a devout Christian and an ordained minister. Early in his career, after only eighteen amateur fights, Foreman won the Olympic gold medal as a heavyweight in 1968. He became a professional boxer after the Olympics and eventually won enough fights to shoot for the heavyweight title. Foreman won the title in 1973. From there, he continued his successful boxing career, coming in and out of retirement and winning numerous bouts. Later, he became a commentator for HBO and continues to travel the world to promote his companies.

AL GREEN

Reverend Al Green spent much of his career as both a secular artist and a gospel superstar. Born in 1946 in Arkansas, Green began singing gospel at age nine with his brothers. He later formed the group Al Green and the Soul-mates and produced nationally-acclaimed songs with that group. Al Green continued a distinguished gospel and secular music career, and was inducted into the Rock and Roll Hall of Fame in 1995.

A. V. GRISWOLD

Born as Wana Hobah, in Cape Palmas, Africa in 1836, A.V. Griswold was the son of the king of the Barbo tribe. Griswold was educated by missionaries, whose intent was to teach him their language so that he could translate and print materials for his own people. A fast learner, Griswold soon read and spoke plainly and without embarrassment. It is said that his Bible was his chief companion, and that he was often found praying to God in secret. Sadly, he died due to an inflammation of his lungs. He was only a teenager at the time of his death.

FRED HAMMOND

Fred Hammond is a producer, singer, and instrumentalist in the gospel music arena. Born and raised in Detroit, Michigan, Hammond began singing with his church choir at the age of twelve. Later, he began singing as a member of the group, Commissioned. During their career, the group released numerous albums. Hammond subsequently began a solo career in 1991. Inspirational as a writer and engaging a worship leader, Hammond continues to reach hearts and minds all over the world with the gospel message.

JOSEPHINE DELPHINE HENDERSON HEARD

Josephine Heard was the wife of the great preacher, William Henry Heard. Born shortly after the Civil War began, Josephine was raised by parents committed to education. She was reading by the age of five and grew up to be an educator and prolific poet. Her best-known work was *Morning Glories*, which was written with youth in mind. She died around 1921 in Philadelpia.

JOSIAH HENSON

Born a slave in 1789, Henson was sold numerous times before reaching adulthood. Despite the hardship, he was able to save enough money to purchase his freedom by the age of forty-one. Yet, after presenting the money for his freedom, he was informed that the price had gone up. At this news, Henson decided to escape slavery to Canada. His life inspired the best-selling novel, *Uncle Tom's Cabin*, by Harriet Beecher Stowe.

HOWARD HEWITT

Howard Hewitt grew up in Akron, Ohio. From a stint as a dancer for the hit television series, *Soul Train*, Hewitt quickly advanced to become a vocalist for the rhythm and blues group, Shalamar. The group produced numerous hits before Hewitt embarked on his solo career in 1985. As a devout Christian, Hewitt continues to work as a producer, writer, and session vocalist.

EVANDER HOLYFIELD

Born in 1962, the youngest of nine children, Evander Holyfield grew to prominence as a boxer when he won the National Golden Gloves championship and earned a place on the United States

Olympic team in the early 1980s. From there, he rose in the boxing ranks until he fulfilled his dream of becoming the heavyweight champion of the world in 1990, defeating James "Buster" Douglas. Holyfield has been champion a of Christian causes around the world and is the founder of the Holyfield foundation, which helps disadvantaged children.

GEORGE M. HORTON

George Moses Horton was born in 1797. He was a slave who taught himself to read and later became a poet. As a teenager, he frequented the University of North Carolina to sell his poetic and acrostic works to students for the cost of twenty-five and seventy-five cents. This, along with his work as a campus laborer, bought his freedom. Horton wrote the first book published in the South by a black man, *The Hope of Liberty*. With the support of governors, abolitionists, and clergymen, Horton continued writing until his final years. His last days were spent writing Sunday school stories in Philadelphia.

BO JACKSON

Jackson was one of the few athletes to ever participate in both professional baseball and professional football. He started his football career with the Los Angeles Raiders and his baseball career with the Kansas City Royals. Due to an injury and continuing health problems, Jackson stopped playing professional sports in 1994. Even so, he achieved a distinguished career in both sports.

MAHALIA JACKSON

The granddaughter of slaves, Mahalia Jackon was born in 1911 in New Orleans, Louisiana. It is said that she began singing as soon as she started walking and talking. She was raised by an aunt in a very strict Christian household, the foundation on which she would build her career as a gospel singer. Jackson was almost single-handedly responsible for bringing gospel music to the forefront of the African-American music scene of her day. By blending the lyrics of gospel with a blues melody, Jackson took the world by storm, becoming world-renowned as a vocalist. She was invited to sing in churches across the country, from New York to California. She was also active in the Civil Rights Movement and sang just before Martin Luther King Jr. gave his famous "I Have a Dream" speech in 1963. In her later years, Jackson struggled with illness and eventually succumbed to a heart condition in 1972.

PRAYING JACOB

Known only as Praying Jacob, this man was written about in the *Narrative of the Life and Labors of the Rev. G.W. Offley.* Jacob had such an intimate relationship with God that even his slave masters recognized it.

PHEBE ANN JACOBS

Phebe Ann Jacobs was a coloured woman born a slave in Morris County, New Jersey, July 1785. At an early age she was given to Mrs. Wheelock, wife of President Wheelock of Dartmouth College, to be an attendant on her daughter, Maria Malleville, who was afterwards the wife of President Allen of Bowdoin College, Brunswick, Maine. She came to Brunswick with President Allen's family in 1820 and remained with them until the death of Mrs. Allen, after which she chose to live alone. She died in Brunswick on February 28, 1850.

T. D. JAKES

Born in 1957, Thomas Dexter Jakes grew up in West Virginia, where he was raised in the Baptist church and eventually served as a music director. In his first pastoral position at Greater Emmanuel

Temple of Faith, Jakes had an initial congregation of ten people. However, Jakes rose to prominence with his ground-breaking book, *Woman Thou Art Loosed*, which was initially self-published but went on to become a national best-seller. Jakes eventually moved to Texas, where he started The Potter's House Church in Dallas. He now leads a congregation of over 17,000 members. Known around the world as T.D. Jakes, he continues to inspire and change lives through his impassioned gospel messages.

JOHN JASPER

At the time of his conversion John Jasper was a slave, illiterate and working in a tobacco factory in Richmond. Jasper was unmatched in his presentation of the Gospel. His tall stature, his commanding tone, even his broken English contributed to his ability to be used of God to reach both blacks and whites with the message of God's word. Though born a slave in 1812, Jasper taught himself to read and spent his entire life bringing God-breathed messages until his death in 1912.

JOHN JEA

Writer, poet, and preacher John Jea was born in Old Callabar, Africa in the year 1773. Stolen from the African continent and brought to America as a slave, Jea was taught by his master that Africans had no God at all. Because of this, according to his own account, Jea lived his earlier years in all types of sinful living, even as a slave. However, Jea became greatly impacted by a sermon and God began to deal strongly with him about his sins. His conversion was so great that he was able to look certain death in the face without fear. Such boldness was useful to him in his career as a traveling preacher who went as far away as the East Indies, Ireland, and England where he pastured a small house church.

ALAN KEYES

Alan Keyes was born into a military family and spent much of his childhood in bases across the United States and Italy. He attended Cornell University but later transferred to Harvard University. Keyes earned his Ph.D. in government policy and began working with the U.S. State Department in 1978. Serving under President Reagan, Keyes often took on controversial positions that were not condoned by prominent black leaders of the day. However, Keyes persevered and eventually started a radio talk show called America's Wake up Call: The Alan Keyes Show. Then, in 1995, Keyes became the first black Republican Presidential candidate. Keyes captured the attention of Christians all over the country and his run garnered much-needed attention. He also made a second bid for the presidency in 1999-2000, one of three finalists, leaving him to debate Senator John McCain and future President George W. Bush.

MARTIN LUTHER KING JR.

Believed by many to be the face of the modern Civil Rights Movement, Martin Luther King Jr. was one of many who banded together to end segregation in the South. Having come from a family of Baptist ministers, King worked tirelessly until his death to fight for civil equality. He entered Morehouse College at only 15 years old and there received his B.A. He later received his divinity degree at Crozer Theological Seminary. King's civil rights actions began in Montgomery, Alabama, where a woman named Rosa Parks had been arrested for not giving up her seat for a white man. The response to this atrocity was overwhelming and the Civil Rights Movement began in earnest. Martin Luther King Jr. became a voice to blacks across the nation. He fought for the rights of African Americans through boycotts, speeches, and political support from those who were in favor of the rights of the black community. He strove for racial justice until his tragic assassination in April of 1968.

LUCY LARCOM

Lucy Larcom was born in Beverly, Massachusetts in 1826. She was a writer of patriotic poems during the Civil War and penned numerous poetic works throughout her life.

JARENA LEE

Jarena Lee overcame all odds to become an ordained preacher in the early 19th century. Despite widespread opposition to her ministry, she became a well-known exhorter.

CARL LEWIS

World Champion track runner Carl Lewis was born in Wilingboro, New Jersey. After suffering complications related to a sudden growth spurt at the age of fifteen, Lewis had to walk on crutches for nearly a month. Just one year after those physical complications, Lewis ran the hundred-meter dash in just ten seconds. Carl Lewis attended the University of Houston and won numerous championships in the long jump. Soon after that Lewis joined the Santa Monica Track Club, which paved his way to the Olympics. At the 1984 Olympics, he made history by duplicating Jesse Owens' accomplishment of winning gold medals in the hundred-meter, two-hundred meter, long jump, and the 4 by 100-meter relay. During the one-hundred meter, he was clocked at nearly thirty miles-per-hour and won the race by almost eight feet.

NELSON MANDELA

Nelson Rolihlahla Mandela was born in Transkei, South Africa on July 18, 1918. His father was Chief Henry Mandela of the Tembu Tribe. Mandela himself was educated at University College of Fort Hare and the University of Witwatersrand and qualified in law in 1942. He joined the African National Congress (ANC) in 1944 and was engaged in resistance against the ruling National Party's apartheid policies after 1948. During his years in prison, Nelson Mandela's reputation grew steadily. He was widely accepted as the most significant black leader in South Africa and became a potent symbol of resistance as the anti-apartheid movement gathered strength. He consistently refused to compromise his political position to obtain his freedom. Nelson Mandela was released on February 18, 1990. In 1991, at the first national conference of the ANC held inside South Africa after the organization had been banned in 1960, Mandela was elected President of the ANC while his lifelong friend and colleague, Oliver Tambo, became the organization's National Chairperson.[1]

MARY F. MCCRAY

Mary McCray was born on May 26, 1837. Her narrative, written by her husband and son, was about her life and conversion. Her life was solely about her Lord. McCray's life was defined by a vision she received that led her into her calling and true conversion. She later went from house to house leading prayer meetings and ministering the gospel.

OTIS MOSS

The Rev. Dr. Otis Moss is the pastor of the Olivet Institutional Baptist Church in Cleveland, Ohio. Born in Georgia, Moss was educated at Morehouse College. He was heavily involved in the Civil Rights Movement and was a religious leader for more than thirty years. He also served as a co-pastor with Dr. Martin Luther King, Sr. at the Ebenezer Baptist Church in Atlanta, Georgia.

JESSE OWENS

Jesse Owens was born in 1913 in Oakville, Alabama. His athletic ability became evident when, in junior high, he jumped six feet in the high jump and over twenty-two feet in the long jump. He continued to win major track events during high school and college. Owens disproved Adolph Hitler's theories of white supremacy when he won four gold medals in the 1936 Berlin Olympics on behalf of the United States. After this glorious event, he returned to America and was forced to do odd jobs to support his family. After taking a job as a playground director, he began championing the causes of disadvantaged youth. He became a board member of the Chicago Boy's Club. Later, he was named by the State Department as the US Ambassador of Sports. This helped him further his cause on behalf of disadvantaged youth. Later in life, he was presented with the Living Legend award from President Jimmy Carter. After his death, he was also honored by President George Bush with the Congressional Gold Medal, which was presented to his wife, Ruth S. Owens.

ROSA PARKS

Rosa Parks has been called the mother of the modern Civil Rights movement. Born Rosa Louise McCauley in 1913, Parks was raised by her mother and grandparents. She attended segregated schools and studied at Alabama State College. While riding home from work one day, Parks refused to give up her seat for a white man in the segregated city bus and was arrested. The black community in the South was outraged and soon began a boycott of the transit system under the leadership of the young minister, Reverend Martin Luther King, Jr.

ANN PLATO

The author of the acclaimed, *Essays; Including Biographies and Miscellaneous Pieces, in Prose and Poetry,* Ann Plato was born in 1820. Her book was the second book published by a black woman in America. She was a devout member of the Colored Congregational Church of Hartford, Connecticut, and was highly esteemed by the abolitionists and church leaders of her day.

PETER RANDOLPH

Peter Randolph was a newspaper editor and Baptist minister in Richmond, Virginia. Born a slave, Randolph received his freedom upon his master's death. He wrote his autobiography entitled, *From the Slave Cabin to the Pulpit.*

H. CORDELIA RAY

Ray had one goal – to make her mark in literature. And that she did, after graduating with multiple degrees and teaching for many years in the New York City public school system. She is the author of her father's biography, *A Sketch of the Life of Reverend Charles B. Ray.* Her work also appeared in numerous periodicals. *Sonnets*, a book of poems, was her best known work and was published in 1910.

CONDOLEEZA RICE

Condoleezza Rice was born in Birmingham, Alabama in 1954. She is the first black female National Security Advisor of the United States. She earned her bachelor's degree in political science, cum laude and Phi Beta Kappa, from the University of Denver in 1974; her master's from the University of Notre Dame in 1975; and her Ph.D. from the Graduate School of International Studies at the University of Denver in 1981. Rice is a fellow of the American Academy of Arts and Sciences and has been awarded honorary doctorates from Morehouse College in 1991, the University of Alabama in 1994, the University of Notre Dame in 1995, the Mississippi College School of Law in 2003, the University of Louisville and Michigan State University in 2004. During her career, Rice has served on the board of directors in numerous corporations, received numerous honors as an outstanding professor, and served for six years as Stanford University's Provost.

DAVID ROBINSON

Born in Key West, Florida in 1965, and known by his fans as the Admiral, David Robinson had a distinguished career in the NBA. A 9-time all-star player, Robinson stayed with the San Antonio Spurs throughout his NBA career. He was named one of the 50 greatest NBA basketball players of all time. Robinson is now an author and champion of numerous Christian and social causes.

JACKIE ROBINSON

Jackie Robinson was born in Cairo, Georgia in 1919. Jackie Robinson broke the color line when he became the first black major league baseball player after signing a contract with the Brooklyn Dodgers in 1947. This event rocked the world of baseball and paved the way for many other great African-American ballplayers.

BARRY SANDERS

Barry Sanders was born in 1968. He is a Heisman trophy winner from Oklahoma State University and holds the all-time NCAA record for single-season rushing. After college, Sanders joined the NFL, where he became one of the most thrilling running backs in history. He was inducted into the Pro Football Hall of Fame in 2004.

EFFIE WALLER SMITH

Effie Waller Smith was born in 1879 in Kentucky. She began writing at sixteen years old and authored numerous books. Her work was featured in several major magazines of her day. However, due to the racial issues of that time, much of her work has gone largely unacknowledged. Although Effie died in obscurity in 1906, her work lives on as a voice of hope to future generations.

MARIA STEWART

Maria Stewart was born in Connecticut in 1803. Despite humble beginnings, her life had great impact. She devoted her life to being a preacher, political activist, and abolitionist. For her, character was a central issue if blacks were ever to be viewed as equals in the racist society of her day. She lived out the last years of her life as a teacher and continued writing to further her cause.

CLARA ANN THOMPSON

As a child of former slaves, Clara Ann Thompson grew up with a passion for the art of poetry. Having published a number of works, her best-known was *Songs from the Wayside*, which was an overtly religious and theological work, published in 1900. Clara Ann died in 1949.

THEODORE TILTON

Tilton was a journalist and editor-in-chief of the *Independent*, a Congregationalist publication. He was an active supporter and parishoner of Henry Ward Beecher, who was a preacher and abolitionist.

CHARLES TINDLEY

Charles Tindley was an Episcopal minister, and is considered by many as the father of gospel music. Born in 1851 in Maryland, the son of slaves, Tindley taught himself to read and write. He did not need much more in order to become one of the most prolific African-American songwriters of his time. He wrote nearly 50 songs in all, some of which are still sung in churches today.

SOJOURNER TRUTH

Born a slave named Isabella Baumfree, she escaped slavery prior to the emancipation of slaves in New York. After accepting her call to preach, Isabella changed her name to Sojourner Truth and began crusading for the rights of blacks and women. She is most famous for her "Ain't I a Woman" speech, but is also known for being a fiery and uncompromising preacher of the Gospel. Standing nearly six feet tall and known for her booming voice, Sojourner Truth's words touched the hearts of her audience with a message that did not ask for, but demanded, freedom and liberty for all under God.

HARRIET TUBMAN

Harriet Tubman, perhaps more than any other slave, put her own life in danger for the cause of freedom. Often called Moses by those she helped to free, Tubman was born a slave with the name of Araminta around 1820. During the Civil War, Tubman worked as a nurse and a spy for the Union army. She developed the secret routes and shelters in the homes of abolitionists that made up the Underground Railroad, helping to secure the freedom of hundreds of slaves between 1850 to 1860. Later in her life, she became involved in the abolitionist cause, working tirelessly with historical figures such as Susan B. Anthony, Frederick Douglass, and Ralph Waldo Emerson until her death in 1913.

DESMUND TUTU

Archbishop Desmond Tutu was born in 1931 in Klerksdorp, Transvaal. His father was a teacher and he himself was educated at Johannesburg Bantu High School. After leaving school, Archbishop Tutu trained first as a teacher at Pretoria Bantu Normal College and in 1954 graduated from the University of South Africa. After three years as a high school teacher, he began to study theology, receiving his ordination as a priest in 1960. The years 1962-1966 were devoted to further theological study in England leading up to a master's of theology. From 1967 to 1972 Archbishop Tutu taught theology in South Africa before returning to England to take a position as the assistant director of a theological institute in London. In 1975 he was appointed dean of St. Mary's Cathedral in Johannesburg, the first black to hold that position. From 1976 to 1978 Tutu was Bishop of Lesotho and in 1978 became the first black General Secretary of the South African Council of Churches. Archbishop Tutu is an honorary doctor of a number of leading universities in the USA, Britain, and Germany.[2]

CICELY TYSON

Cicely Tyson was born in New York City in 1933, and began her career as a model after being discovered in a beauty salon. Later, she embarked upon a career as a film, television, and stage actress. Her first real break came when she played a secretary in the television series *East Side / West Side*. She also starred in the soap opera *Guiding Light*. Her best-known role was her Oscar-nominated performance in the film, *Sounder*.

HERSCHEL WALKER

As a child, Walker showed little interest in football, preferring to read books and write poetry. But at age twelve, he began to exercise and increased in both strength and speed. By the time he reached high school, he was playing football, basketball and running track. In football, he became a record-breaking running back and led his team to several State Championships, while maintaining above-average grades. He later played for the University of Georgia and the Dallas Cowboys. Arguably one of the greatest running backs of all time, Walker gained more yards in his career than any previous NFL player.

BOOKER T. WASHINGTON

Booker T. Washington was born a slave is Hale's Ford, Virginia in 1856. His family was so poor that he began working at the age of nine as a coal and salt miner. After working for years during his childhood, he quit work to go to school. At sixteen years of age, Washington walked 200 miles to get to the Hampton Institute and paid his own tuition by working as a janitor. Washington believed that education and the ability to make money would raise blacks to equality in this country. He felt that character, integrity, study, and hard work were the things that would cause the black race to excel and rise to prominence. Washington became a teacher and later founded the Tuskegee Normal and Industrial Institute in Tuskegee, Alabama.

J. C. WATTS

J.C. Watts was born in Eufala, Oklahoma in 1957. He attended the University of Oklahoma, where he earned a bachelor's degree in journalism. Watts was also a quarterback for the Oklahoma Sooners, leading them to two consecutive championships. He was also selected as the most valuable player in the 1980 and 1981 Orange Bowl. After college, Watts went on to serve as a youth pastor at Sunnylane Baptist Church and soon became associate pastor. Watts later began public life, running for Congress in 1994 and winning with fifty-two percent of the vote. He served four terms in Congress and continued to grow in prominence in both public and private life. Known as a man of great character and passionate convictions, J.C. Watts now serves as one of the most important African-American voices of the day.

PHYLLIS WHEATLEY

Phyllis Wheatley was born around 1753 in West Africa. She was captured and brought to New England as a young girl between 6 and 8 years old. Miraculously, this young girl lived through the dangerous journey across the Atlantic. Upon arrival in New England, she was purchased by John Wheatley, a businessman from Boston. She learned to read and write and was treated relatively well in the Wheatley household. Once she started writing, there was no stopping her. She became fluent in Latin and was able to interpret even the most difficult Bible verses. Phyllis was freed from slavery in 1774 and married, but was abandoned by her husband only a few years afterward. Although she died at only thirty-one years of age she impacted the lives of thousands with her written works.

OURAGE

WAIT ON THE LORD: BE OF GOOD COURAGE,
AND HE SHALL STRENGTHEN THINE HEART:
WAIT, I SAY, ON THE LORD.

PSALM 27:14

But I wasn't going to give up—the word "quit" has never been part of my vocabulary. With lots of hard work, determination, perseverance and faith in God, I was able to resume training and regain my health. In 1992, less than 17 months after the doctors had considered amputating my feet, I won my first gold medal in the 100-meter dash at the Olympics in Barcelona, Spain, and was named the "World's Fastest Woman." I knew I was back!

—GAIL DEVERS[3]

I knew that God did not put me on the face of this earth to bang on a typewriter for the rest of my life. I don't know what or where it is, but I am going to find it.

—CICELY TYSON[4]

HYMN TO THE MORNING

PHYLLIS WHEATLEY

ATTEND my lays, ye ever honored Nine,
Assist my labors, and my strains refine;
In smoothest numbers pour the notes along,
For bright Aurora now demands my song.

Aurora hail! And all the thousand dies,
Which deck thy progress through the vaulted skies:
The morn awakes, and wide extends her rays,
On ev'ry leaf the gentle zephyr plays;
Harmonious lays the feathered race resume,
Dart the bright eye, and shake the painted plume.

Ye shady groves, your verdant bloom display,
To shield your poet from the burning day:
Calliope, awake the sacred lyre,
While thy fair sisters fan the pleasing fire.
The bowers, the gales, the variegated skies,
In all their pleasures in my bosom rise.

See in the east, the illustrious king of day!
His rising radiance drives the shades away—
But oh! I feel His fervid beams too strong,
And scarce begun, concludes the abortive song.[5]

GIVE EAR TO MY WORDS, O LORD, CONSIDER MY MEDITATION.
HEARKEN UNTO THE VOICE OF MY CRY, MY KING, AND MY GOD:
FOR UNTO THEE WILL I PRAY. MY VOICE SHALT THOU HEAR IN
THE MORNING, O LORD; IN THE MORNING WILL I DIRECT MY
PRAYER UNTO THEE, AND WILL LOOK UP.

—PSALM 5:1-3

HYMN TO THE EVENING

PHYLLIS WHEATLEY

Soon as the sun forsook the eastern main,
The pealing thunder shook the heavenly plain;
Majestic grandeur! From the zephyr's wing,
Exhales the incense of the blooming spring.
Soft purl the streams, the birds renew their notes,
And through the air their mingled music floats.

Through all the heavens what beauteous dyes are spread,
But the west glories in the deepest red:
So may our breasts with ev'ry virtue glow,
The living temples of our God below!
Filled with the praise of Him who gives the light,
And draws the sable curtains of the night.

Let placid slumbers soothe each weary mind,
At morn to wake, more heavenly, more refined;
So shall the labours of the day begin
More pure, more guarded from the snares of sin.
Night's leaden scepter seals my drowsy eyes,
Then cease my song, till fair Aurora rise.[6]

PRAYING JACOB

The following story illustrates the power of Christ to overcome even the most difficult trials. Yet, those hardships, as in this case, can be overcome by fervent prayer and endurance.

Our family theology teaches that God is no respecter of persons, but He gave His Son to die for all, bond or free, black or white, rich or poor. If we keep His commandments, we will be happy after death. It also teaches that if God calls and sanctifies a person to do some great work, that person is immortal until his work is done; that God is able and will protect him from all danger or accident in life if he is faithful to his calling or charge committed by the Lord. This is a borrowed idea from circumstances too numerous to mention.

Here is one man we present as a proof of the immortality of man, while in the flesh: Praying Jacob. This man was a slave in the state of Maryland. His master was very cruel to his slaves. Jacob's rule was to pray three times a day, at just such an hour of the day; no matter what his work was or where he might be, he would stop and go and pray. His master had been to him and pointed his gun at him, and told him if he did not cease praying he would blow out his brains. Jacob would finish his prayer and then tell his master to shoot and welcome, saying "your loss will be my gain. I have two masters—one on earth and one in heaven—Master Jesus in heaven, and Master Saunders on earth. I have a soul and a body; the body belongs to you, Master Saunders, and the soul to Master Jesus. Jesus says men ought always to pray, but you will not pray, neither do you want to have me pray."

This man said in private conversation that several times he

went home and drank an unusual quantity of brandy to harden his heart that he might kill him; but he never had power to strike nor shoot him, and he would freely give the world, if he had it in his possession, for what he believed his Jacob to possess. He also thought that Jacob was as sure of Heaven as the apostle Paul or Peter. Sometimes Mr. S. would be in the field about half drunk, raging like a madman, whipping the other slaves; and when Jacob's hour would come for prayer, he would stop his horses and plough and kneel down and pray; but he could not strike the man of God.[7]

WHEN A MAN'S WAYS PLEASE THE LORD, HE MAKETH EVEN HIS ENEMIES TO BE AT PEACE WITH HIM.

—PROVERBS 16:7

A SONG OF THE MAN: HENRY "BOX" BROWN

Here you see a man by the name of Henry Brown,
Ran away from the South to the North;
Which he would not have done but they stole all his rights,
But they'll never do the like again.

Chorus: Brown laid down the shovel and the hoe,
Down in the box he did go;
No more Slave work for Henry "box" Brown,
In the box by Express he did go.

Then the orders they were given, and the cars did start away;
Roll along—roll along—roll along,
Down to the landing, where the steamboat lay,
To bear the baggage off to the north.

CHORUS

When they packed the baggage on, they turned him on his head,
There poor Brown liked to have died;
There were passengers on board who wished to sit down,
And they turned the box down on its side.

CHORUS

When they got to the cars they threw the box off,
And down upon his head he did fall.
Then he heard his neck crack, and he thought it was broke,
But they never threw him off any more.

CHORUS

When they got to Philadelphia they said he was in port,
And Brown then began to feel glad;
He was taken on the wagon to his final destination,
And left, "this side up with care."

CHORUS

The friends gathered round and asked if all was right,
As down on the box they did rap,
Brown answered them, saying; "yes, all is right!"
He was then set free from his pain.

CHORUS[8]

The Bible is very clear: Don't do your good works before
men to be cheered by men. I do the right things because
that's what God told us to do

—DAVID ROBINSON[9]

Fear causes you to do the easy thing, the quickest thing.

—EVANDER HOLYFIELD[10]

FAITH AND HOPE

Blessed is the man that trusteth in the Lord,
and whose hope the Lord is.

Jeremiah 17:7

One reason that genuine believers tend to doubt their salvation is that we don't receive all of it at once. Our full redemption is "reserved in heaven for [us]."

—ANTHONY EVANS[11]

We sometimes let circumstances destroy us rather than having faith in God's mercy and grace, and in the fact that He's going to protect us at all times. We can fall into real crazy areas in our lives if we don't live by faith.

—HOWARD HEWITT[12]

I like to do things well. But I like to keep all of it in perspective. Because ultimately, what matters when you leave this earth are the relationships you leave behind . . . Your religious faith is all that there is to sustain you. Getting too focused on anything else is a problem.

—CONDOLEEZZA RICE[13]

HOPE THOU IN GOD

JOSEPHINE DELPHINE HENDERSON HEARD

O soul, why shouldn't thou downcast be?
Or mourn thy temporal lot;
Where'er 'tis cast, what's that to thee—
Doth not God choose the spot?
Rouse thee, and labor for success!
And be thou well assured;
The shadows near the end grow less,
And pain must be endured.

Although I meet with conflicts here,
And storms beset my path,
Though devils shoot their fiery darts
Of disappointed wrath,
My feet upon the blood-marked way,
Shall ever onward press,
And looking to the "perfect day,"
My faith shall not grow less.

What if the ungodly spread a snare,
And wicked councils meet—
Lord, guard with loving, watchful care,
My timid, faltering feet.

Soul, thou must daily suppliance make,
If thou wouldn't well be fed—
The righteous He will not forsake,
Nor shall His seed beg bread.

The cloudy pillar day by day,
The fiery cloud by night,
Shall mark the straight and narrow path,
That leads to lasting light.
Where trembling hope receives her sight,
Where flowers eternal grow—
God's presence beams forever bright,
And living waters flow.[14]

THOU WILT SHOW ME THE PATH OF LIFE: IN THY PRESENCE IS FULL-
NESS OF JOY; AT THY RIGHT HAND THERE ARE PLEASURES FOR
EVERMORE.

—PSALM 16:11

THE DAUGHTER OF HEAVEN

ANN PLATO

Lift up thy head, O Christian, and look forward to calm, unclouded regions of mercy, unfilled by vapors, unruffled by storms—where celestial friendship, the loveliest form in Heaven, never dies, never changes, never cools! Soon you shall burst this brittle earthly poison of the body, break the fetter of mortality, spring to endless life, and mingle with the skies.

How many of us are able to say that we are persuaded that neither life nor death, nor things present, nor things to come, nor height, nor depth, nor any other creature, shall be able to separate us from the love of God, which is in Christ Jesus, our Lord? Religion confers on the mind principles of noble independence. "The upright man is satisfied from himself"; he despises not the advantages of fortune, but he centers not his happiness in them. With a moderate share of them he can be contented; and contentment is felicity.

Happy in his own integrity, conscious of the esteem of good men, reposing firm trust in providence, and the promises of God, he is exempt from servile dependence on other things. He can wrap himself up in a good conscience, and look forward, without terror, to the change of the world. Let all things fluctuate around him as they please, that by the Divine ordination they shall be made to work together in the issue, for his good; and, therefore, having much to hope from God, and little to fear from the world, he can be easy in every state. One who possesses within himself such an establishment of mind is truly free.

The character of God, as Supreme Ruler of the world, demands our supreme reverence and our cordial and entire obedience to His will. Hence proceeds our duty to worship Him; for worship, external acts of homage, are the means of preserving, in our minds that fear and reverence, a spirit of obedience. Neglect of worshiping God is inevitably followed by forgetfulness of God, and by consequence, a loss of the reverence for His authority, which prompts to obedience.

We know that God is love; and love among men is the fulfillment of the law. Love is the principal source of other virtues, and of all genuine happiness. From a supreme love to God, and from a full persuasion of His perfect benevolence and almighty power, springs confidence—a trusting in Him for protection, for safety, for support, and for final salvation.

This confidence in God, springing from love, implying cordial approbation of His character and obedience to His gospel, is Christian faith. This is the anchor of the soul, sure and steadfast; the foundation of the Christian's hope; it is this alone which sustains the good man amidst all the storms of life, and enables him to meet adversity, in all its forms, with firmness and tranquility.

It is impossible to love God without desiring to please Him, and as far as we are able, to resemble Him; therefore, the love of God must lead to every virtue, in the highest degree. We may be sure we do not truly love Him if we content ourselves with avoiding flagrant sins, and not strive, in good earnest, to reach the greatest degree of perfection of which we are capable. Thus do these few words direct us to the highest Christian virtue. Indeed, the whole tenor of the gospel is to offer us every help, direction, and motive that can enable us to attain that degree of faith on which depends our eternal good.

There are many circumstances in our situation that peculiarly require the support of religion to enable us to act in them with spirit and propriety. Our whole life is often a life of suffering. We can not engage in business or dissipate ourselves in pleasure and riot as irreligious men too often do: We must bear our sorrows in silence, unknown and unpitied. We must often put on a face of serenity and cheerfulness when our hearts are torn with anguish, or sinking in despair.

There is not, in my opinion, a more pleasing and triumphant consideration in religion, than this: of the perpetual progress which the soul makes towards the perfection of its nature without ever arriving at a period in it. To look upon the soul as going on from strength to strength to consider that she is to shine forever with new accessions of glory, and brighten to all eternity; that she will be adding virtue to virtue, and knowledge to knowledge; carries in it something wonderfully agreeable to that ambition which is natural to the mind of man. Nay, it must be pleasing to God himself, to see His creation forever beautifying in His eyes and drawing nearer to Him by greater degrees of resemblance.

With what astonishment and veneration may we look into God's own Word, where there are such hidden stores of virtue and knowledge, such inexhaustible sources of perfection! We know not yet what we shall be; nor has it ever entered into the heart of man to conceive the glory that will be always in reserve for him.

Thus make our lives glide on serenely; and when the angel of death receives his commission to put a period to our existence, may we receive the summons with tranquility, and pass without fear the gloomy valley which separates time from eternity. May we remember that this life is nothing more than a short duration, a prelude to another, which will never have an end.

Happy . . . to whom the present life has no charms for which [you cannot] wish it to be protracted. [Your] troubles will soon vanish like a dream, which mocks the power of memory; and what signify all the shocks which thy feeling spirit can meet with in this transitory world? A few moments longer, and [your] complaints will be forever at an end; [your] disease of body and mind shall be felt no more; the ungenerous hints of churlish relations shall distress, fortune frown, and futurity intimidate no more.

Then shall thy voice, no longer breathing the plaintive strains of melancholy, but happily attend, attuned to songs of gladness, mingle with the hosts, mortals or immortals sung: "O, Death! Where is thy sting? O, Grave! Where is thy victory? Thanks be to God, who [gives] us the victory, through our Lord Jesus Christ; blessing and honor, glory and power, be unto Him that sits upon the throne, and unto the Lamb forever and ever."[15]

LET US HOLD FAST THE PROFESSION OF [OUR] FAITH WITHOUT WAVERING; FOR HE [IS] FAITHFUL THAT PROMISED.

—HEBREWS 10:23

BEAMS OF HEAVEN

CHARLES TINDLEY

Beams of heaven, as I go,
Through this wilderness below,
Guide my feet in peaceful ways;
Turn my midnights into days.
When in the darkness I would grope,
Faith always sees a star of hope.
And soon from all life's grief and danger
I shall be free someday.
I don't know how long 'twill be
Nor for what the future holds for me.

But this I know, if
Jesus leads me
I shall get a home someday.
Oftentimes my sky is clear;
Joy abounds without a tear.
Though a day so bright begun,
Clouds may hide tomorrow's sun.
There'll be a day that's always bright;
A day that never yields to night.
And in its light the streets of glory
I shall behold someday.
Harder yet may be the fight,
Right may often yield to might,
Wickedness awhile may reign,
Satan's cause may seem to gain.
There is a God that rules above
With hand of power and heart of love.
If I am right, He'll fight my battle.
I shall have peace someday.
Burdens now may crush me down,
Disappointments all around,
Troubles speak in mournful sigh,
Sorrow through a tear-stained eye.
There is a world where pleasure reigns.
No mourning soul shall roam its plains,
And to that land of peace and glory
I want to go someday. [16]

FOR VERILY I SAY UNTO YOU, THAT WHOSOEVER SHALL SAY UNTO
THIS MOUNTAIN, BE THOU REMOVED, AND BE THOU CAST INTO THE
SEA; AND SHALL NOT DOUBT IN HIS HEART, BUT SHALL BELIEVE
THAT THOSE THINGS WHICH HE SAITH SHALL COME TO PASS; HE
SHALL HAVE WHATSOEVER HE SAITH.

—MARK 11:23

DOUBT

CLARA ANN THOMPSON

A doubt crept into a heart one day;
The brave heart said, "Twill be gone tomorrow."
Ah, little it knew!
For it steadily grew,
Till it covered that heart with a pall of sorrow;
And there came at length, a darksome day,
When the hope of life seemed gone for aye.

A ray of light, in a darkened heart;
Yes, only a ray, but it grew more bright,
And it steadily spread,
Through darkness and dread,
Till it flooded that heart with a glorious light;
And a soul gave thanks to its God, above;
The light was a Savior's guiding love.[17]

I'll Follow Thee

CLARA ANN THOMPSON

My Saviour, let me hear Thy voice tonight,
I'll follow Thee, I'll follow Thee;
The clouds that overhang my way obscure the light,
And all is dark to me.

I'd hear Thy voice above the tempest's shriek;
I'll follow Thee, I'll follow Thee;
And though my sight be dim, my spirit weak,
I'll trust, though naught I see.

I'd feel Thy arm, supporting in the dark;
I'll follow Thee, I'll follow Thee;
For Thou canst fan to flame faith's sinking spark,
And seal my loyalty.

I shall not sink, dear Lord, when Thou'rt my guide,
I'll follow Thee, I'll follow Thee;
Though lashed by heavy waves on ev'ry side,
I'm safe, when Thou'rt with me. [18]

THE LORD IS MY SHEPHERD; I SHALL NOT WANT. HE MAKETH ME
TO LIE DOWN IN GREEN PASTURES: HE LEADETH ME BESIDE THE
STILL WATERS. HE RESTORETH MY SOUL: HE LEADETH ME IN THE
PATHS OF RIGHTEOUSNESS FOR HIS NAME'S SAKE. YEA, THOUGH I
WALK THROUGH THE VALLEY OF THE SHADOW OF DEATH, I WILL
FEAR NO EVIL: FOR THOU ART WITH ME; THY ROD AND THY STAFF
THEY COMFORT ME. THOU PREPAREST A TABLE BEFORE ME IN THE
PRESENCE OF MINE ENEMIES: THOU ANOINTEST MY HEAD WITH
OIL; MY CUP RUNNETH OVER. SURELY GOODNESS AND MERCY
SHALL FOLLOW ME ALL THE DAYS OF MY LIFE: AND I WILL DWELL
IN THE HOUSE OF THE LORD FOR EVER.

—PSALM 23

THEN SAID JESUS UNTO HIS DISCIPLES, IF ANY MAN WILL COME
AFTER ME, LET HIM DENY HIMSELF, AND TAKE UP HIS CROSS, AND
FOLLOW ME.

—MATTHEW 16:24

JARENA LEE—RELIGIOUS EXPERIENCE

The man who was to speak in the afternoon of that day was
the Rev. Richard Allen, bishop of the African Episcopal Methodists
in America. During the labors of this man that afternoon, I had
come to the conclusion that this is the people to which my heart
unites, and it so happened, that as soon as the service closed he
invited such as felt a desire to flee the wrath to come, to unite on

trial with them—I embraced the opportunity. Three weeks from that day, my soul was gloriously converted to God, under preaching, at the very outset of the sermon. The text was barely pronounced . . . when there appeared to my view, in the center of the heart, one sin; and this was malice against one particular individual, who had strove deeply to injure me, which I resented.

At this discovery I said, "Lord, I forgive every creature." That instant, it appeared to me as if a garment, which had entirely enveloped my whole person, even to my fingers' ends, split at the crown of my head, and was stripped away from me, passing like a shadow from my sight—when the glory of God seemed to cover me in its stead.

That moment, though hundreds were present, I did leap to my feet and declare that God, for Christ's sake, had pardoned the sins of my soul. Great was the ecstasy of my mind, for I felt that not only the sin of malice was pardoned, but all other sins were swept away together. That day was the first when my heart had believed, and my tongue had made confession unto salvation—the first words uttered, a part of that song, which shall fill eternity with its sound, was glory to God.

For a few moments I had power to exhort sinners, and to tell of the wonders and of the goodness of Him who had clothed me with His salvation. During this the minister was silent, until my soul felt its duty had been performed, when he declared another witness of the power of Christ to forgive sins on earth, was manifest in my conversion.[19]

IT SHALL COME TO PASS IN THE LAST DAYS, SAITH GOD, I WILL
POUR OUT OF MY SPIRIT UPON ALL FLESH: AND YOUR SONS AND
YOUR DAUGHTERS SHALL PROPHESY, AND YOUR YOUNG MEN SHALL
SEE VISIONS, AND YOUR OLD MEN SHALL DREAM DREAMS: AND
ON MY SERVANTS AND ON MY HANDMAIDENS I WILL POUR OUT IN
THOSE DAYS OF MY SPIRIT; AND THEY SHALL PROPHESY.

—ACTS 2:17-18

IS GOD DEAD?

It was at a crowded public meeting in Faneuil Hall, where
Frederick Douglass was one of the chief speakers. Douglass had
been describing the wrongs of the black race, and as he proceeded,
he grew more and more excited, and finally ended by saying that
they had no hope of justice from the whites, no possible hope except
in their own right arms. It must come to blood; they must fight for
themselves and redeem themselves, or it would never be done.

Sojourner was sitting, tall and dark, on the very front seat,
facing the platform; and in the hush of deep feeling after Douglass
sat down, she spoke out in her deep, peculiar voice, heard all over
the house,

"Frederick, is God dead?"

The effect was perfectly electrical, and thrilled through the
whole house, changing as by a flash the whole feeling of the audience. Not another word she said or needed to say; it was enough.

WHITHER SHALL I GO FROM THY SPIRIT? OR WHITHER SHALL I FLEE
FROM THY PRESENCE? IF I ASCEND UP INTO HEAVEN, THOU ART
THERE: IF I MAKE MY BED IN HELL, BEHOLD, THOU ART THERE. IF I
TAKE THE WINGS OF THE MORNING, AND DWELL IN THE UTTER-
MOST PARTS OF THE SEA; EVEN THERE SHALL THY HAND LEAD ME,
AND THY RIGHT HAND SHALL HOLD ME.

—PSALM 139:7-10

GOLIATH OF GATH: PART 1

PHYLLIS WHEATLEY

YE martial powers, and all ye tuneful nine,
Inspire my song, and aid my high design.
The dreadful scenes and toils of war I write,
The ardent warriors and the fields of fight:
You best remember, and you best can sing
The acts of heroes to the vocal string:
Resume the lays with which your sacred lyre,
Did then the poet and the sage inspire.

Now front to front the armies were displayed,
Here Israel ranged, and there the foes arrayed;
The hosts on two opposing mountains stood,
Thick as the foliage of the waving wood:

Between them an extensive valley lay,
O'er which the gleaming armour poured the day;
When, from the camp of the Philistine foes,
Dreadful to view, a mighty warrior rose;
In the dire deeds of bleeding battle skilled,
The monster stalks, the terror of the field.
From Gath he sprung, Goliath was his name,
Of fierce deportment and gigantic frame:
A brazen helmet on his head was placed,
A coat of mail his form terrific graced;
The greaves his legs, the targe his shoulders prest:
Dreadful in arms, high towering o'er the rest,
A spear he proudly waved, whose iron head,
Strange to relate, six hundred shekels weighed:
He strode along, and shook the ample field,
While Phoebus blazed refulgent on his shield.
Through Jacob's race a chilling horror ran,
When thus the huge, enormous chief began:

"Say, what the cause, that in this proud array,
"You set your battle in the face of day?
"One hero find in all your vaunting train,
"Then see who loses, and who wins the plain;
"For he who wins, in triumph may demand
"Perpetual service from the vanquished land:
"Your armies I defy, your force despise,

"By far inferior in Philistia's eyes:
"Produce a man, and let us try the fight,
"Decide the contest, and the victor's right."

Thus challenged he: all Israel stood amazed,
     And ev'ry chief in consternation gazed;
     But Jesse's son, in youthful bloom appears,
     And warlike courage far beyond his years;
     He left the folds, he left the flow'ry meads,
     And soft recesses of the sylvan shades.
     Now Israel's monarch and his troops arise,
     With peals of shouts ascending to the skies;
     In Elab's vale, the scene of combat lies.

When the fair morning blushed with orient red,
     What David's sire enjoined, the son obeyed;
     And swift of foot towards the trench he came,
Where glowed each bosom with the martial flame.
     He leaves his carriage to another's care,
     And runs to greet his brethren of the war.
     While yet they spake the giant chief arose,
     Repeats the challenge, and insults his foes:
Struck with the sound, and trembling at the view,
     Affrighted Israel from its post withdrew.

"Observe ye this tremendous foe," they cry'd,

"Who in proud vaunts our armies hath defy'd.
"Whoever lays him prostrate on the plain,
"Freedom in Israel for his house shall gain;
"And on him wealth unknown the king will pour,
"And give his royal daughter for his dower."[20]

AS HE TALKED WITH THEM, BEHOLD, THERE CAME UP THE CHAMPI-
ON, THE PHILISTINE OF GATH, GOLIATH BY NAME, OUT OF THE
ARMIES OF THE PHILISTINES, AND SPAKE ACCORDING TO THE SAME
WORDS: AND DAVID HEARD THEM. THIS DAY WILL THE LORD
DELIVER THEE INTO MINE HAND; AND I WILL SMITE THEE, AND
TAKE THINE HEAD FROM THEE; AND I WILL GIVE THE CARCASES OF
THE HOST OF THE PHILISTINES THIS DAY UNTO THE FOWLS OF THE
AIR, AND TO THE WILD BEASTS OF THE EARTH; THAT ALL THE
EARTH MAY KNOW THAT THERE IS A GOD IN ISRAEL. AND ALL
THIS ASSEMBLY SHALL KNOW THAT THE LORD SAVETH NOT WITH
SWORD AND SPEAR: FOR THE BATTLE IS THE LORD'S, AND HE WILL
GIVE YOU INTO OUR HANDS.

—1 SAMUEL 17:23, 46-47

The world is a severe schoolmaster, for its frowns are less
dangerous than its smiles and flatteries, and it is a diffi-
cult task to keep in the path of wisdom.

—PHILLIS WHEATLEY (1753-1784)
LETTER TO JOHN THORNTON, OCTOBER 30, 1774

GOLIATH OF GATH: PART 2

PHYLLIS WHEATLEY

Then Jesse's youngest hope: "My brethren, say,
"What shall be done for him who takes away
"Reproach from Jacob, who destroys the chief,
"And puts a period to his country's grief?
"He vaunts the honours of his arms abroad,
"And scorns the armies of the living God."

Thus spoke the youth; the attentive people eyed
The wondrous hero, and again reply'd:
"Such the rewards our monarch will bestow
"On him who conquers and destroys his foe."

Eliab heard, and kindled into ire,
To hear his shepherd brother thus inquire,
And thus begun: "What errand brought thee, say,
"Who keeps thy flock? Or does it go astray?
"I know the base ambition of thine heart,
"But back in safety from the field depart."

Eliab thus, to Jesse's youngest heir,
Expressed his wrath in accents most severe.
When to his brother mildly he reply'd,

"What have I done or what the cause to chide?"

The words were told before the king, who sent
        For the young hero to his royal tent.
        Before the monarch, dauntless, he began;
        "For this Philistine, fail no heart of man:
        "I'll take the vale, and with the giant fight:
        "I dread not all his boasts nor all his might."
When thus the king: "Durst thou, a stripling, go,
        "And venture combat with so great a foe,
        "Who all his days has been inured to fight,
        "And made its deeds his study and delight?
"Battles and bloodshed brought the monster forth,
"And clouds and whirlwinds ushered in his birth."

        When David thus: "I kept the fleecy care,
        "And out there rushed a lion and a bear:
        "A tender lamb the hungry lion took,
        "And with no other weapon than my crook,
        "Bold I pursued, and chased him o'er the field,
        "The prey delivered, and the lion killed.
        "As thus the lion and the bear I slew,
        "So shall Goliath fall, and all his crew:
"The God who saved me from these beasts of prey,
        "By me this monster in the dust shall lay."

So David spoke. The wondering king reply'd;
"Go thou, with heaven and victory on thy side:
"This coat of mail, this sword, gird on," he said,
And placed a mighty helmet on his head.
The coat, the sword, the helm, he laid aside,
Nor chose to venture with those arms untry'd;
Then took his staff, and to the neighbouring brook
Instant he ran, and thence five pebbles took.
Meantime descended to Philistia's son
A radiant cherub, and he thus begun:

"Goliath, well thou know'st thou hast defy'd
"Yon Hebrew armies, and their God deny'd.
"Rebellious wretch! audacious worm! forbear,
"Nor tempt the vengeance of their God too far:
"Them who with His omnipotence contend,
"No eye shall pity and no arm defend.
"Proud as thou art, in short-lived glory great,
"I come to tell thee thine approaching fate.
"Regard my words. The Judge of all the gods,
"Beneath whose steps the tow'ring mountain nods,
"Will give thine armies to the savage brood,
"That cut the liquid air, or range the wood.
"Thee, too, a well aimed pebble shall destroy,
"And thou shalt perish by a beardless boy.
"Such is the mandate from the realms above,

"And, should I try the vengeance to remove,
"Myself a rebel to my king would prove.
"Goliath, say, shall grace to him be shown,
"Who dares heaven's monarch, and insults His throne?"

"Your words are lost on me," the giant cries,
While fear and wrath contended in his eyes;
When thus the messenger from heaven replies:
"Provoke no more Jehovah's awful hand
"To hurl its vengeance on thy guilty land:
"He grasps the thunder, and he wings the storm,
"Servants, their sov'reign's orders to perform."[21]

NO WEAPON THAT IS FORMED AGAINST THEE SHALL PROSPER; AND EVERY TONGUE THAT SHALL RISE AGAINST THEE IN JUDGMENT THOU SHALT CONDEMN. THIS IS THE HERITAGE OF THE SERVANTS OF THE LORD, AND THEIR RIGHTEOUSNESS IS OF ME, SAITH THE LORD.

—ISAIAH 54:17

UNITY

BEHOLD, HOW GOOD AND HOW PLEASANT IT IS
FOR BRETHREN TO DWELL TOGETHER IN UNITY.

PSALM 133:1

It does not matter that board rooms are integrated. It does matter that Stanford and Yale and Harvard are integrated. It's one thing to say that we still have a long way to go, to not be a divided society . . . but it is inaccurate and I think harmful to say that nothing has changed. Do all of us harbor certain racial attitudes? Absolutely. But if you walk into any setting, you will see blacks and whites working side by side, talking about the latest football games, talking to their kids. Most people want this to work. And I think Americans are pretty remarkable in that way.

—Condoleezza Rice[22]

In Africa, you never say, "I am my brother's keeper." You just keep him.

—John Henrik Clarke [23]

I believe that all men, black and brown and white, are brothers, varying through time and opportunity, in form and gift and feature, but differing in no essential particular, and alike in soul and the possibility of infinite development.

—W. E. B. DuBois[24]

We must all learn to live together as brothers, or we will perish together as fools.

—MARTIN LUTHER KING JR.[25]

When will we learn that human beings are of infinite value because they have been created in the image of God, that it is blasphemy to treat them as if they were less than this, and to do so ultimately recoils on those who do this? In dehumanizing others, they are themselves dehumanized. Perhaps oppression dehumanizes the oppressor as much as, if not more than, the oppressed. They need each other to become truly free, to become human. We can be human only in fellowship, in community, in koinonia, in peace . . . . Let us work to be peacemakers, those given a wonderful share in our Lord's ministry of reconciliation. If we want peace, so we have been told, let us work for justice. Let us beat our swords into plowshares . . . . God calls us to be fellow workers with Him so that we can extend His kingdom of shalom, of justice, of goodness, of compassion, of caring, of sharing, of laughter, joy and reconciliation, so that the kingdoms of this world will become the Kingdom of our God and of His Christ, and He shall reign forever and ever. Amen. Then there will be fulfillment of the wonderful vision in the Revelation of St. John the Divine (Revelation 7:9).

—DESMOND TUTU[26]

Let the strivings of us all prove Martin Luther King Jr. to have been correct when he said that humanity can no longer be tragically bound to the starless midnight of racism and war. Let the efforts of us all prove that he was not a mere dreamer when he spoke of the beauty of genuine brotherhood and peace being more precious than diamonds or silver or gold.

—NELSON MANDELA[27]

In all things that are purely social, we can be as separate as the fingers, yet one as the hand in all things essential to mutual progress.

—BOOKER T. WASHINGTON[28]

I would like to be known as a person who is concerned about freedom and equality and justice and prosperity for all people.

—ROSA PARKS[29]

COMFORT

IF THERE BE THEREFORE ANY CONSOLATION IN CHRIST,
IF ANY COMFORT OF LOVE, IF ANY FELLOWSHIP OF THE SPIRIT,
IF ANY BOWELS AND MERCIES, FULFILL YE MY JOY,
THAT YE BE LIKEMINDED, HAVING THE SAME LOVE,
BEING OF ONE ACCORD, OF ONE MIND.

PHILIPPIANS 2:1-2

HOW I GOT OVER

MAHALIA JACKSON

Tell me how I made it over "LORD, GOD, LORD"
Falling and rising all these years.
You know my soul, look back and wonder,
How did I make it over?
I'm gonna wear a diamond garment
In that new Jerusalem, I'm gonna walk the streets of gold.
It's the homeland of the soul.
I'm gonna view the host in white;
They've been traveling day and night,
Coming up from every nation.
They're on their way to the great Cognation
Coming from the north, south, east, and west,
On their way to a land of rest.
And they're gonna join the heavenly choir.
You know we're gonna sing and never get tired,
And then we're gonna sing somewere 'round God's alter,
And then we're gonna shout all our troubles over.
You know we gotta thank God and thank Him for being
So good to me.[30]

"THE LORD HIMSELF SHALL DESCEND FROM HEAVEN WITH A SHOUT, WITH THE VOICE OF THE ARCHANGEL, AND WITH THE TRUMP OF GOD: AND THE DEAD IN CHRIST SHALL RISE FIRST: THEN WE WHICH ARE ALIVE AND REMAIN SHALL BE CAUGHT UP TOGETHER WITH THEM IN THE CLOUDS, TO MEET THE LORD IN THE AIR: AND SO SHALL WE EVER BE WITH THE LORD. WHEREFORE COMFORT ONE ANOTHER WITH THESE WORDS."

—1 THESSALONIANS 4:16-18

WHEN LOVE CALLS YOU HOME

FRED HAMMOND

Waiting on the edge of your prodigal heart,
Waiting for someone to save you from yourself.
Out there on the edge dangling somewhere in the darkness,
Doubting if anybody really cares.
But when Love reached through the shadows,
Whispering your name,
And nothing will ever be the same again.
For when Love calls you home,
Forgiveness embraces a past you once owned.
And all the mistakes that carried your name are gone.
'Cuz that's what happens when Love calls you home.
Cradled in Your mercy that has no limit,
I've finally found a place where I belong.

Now I can't imagine one moment without You in it.
It's hard to believe I tried to make it on my own.
But You picked me up from the ruins of my broken life,
And when every chance was spent You gave me one more try.[31]

I WILL NOT LEAVE YOU COMFORTLESS: I WILL COME TO YOU. YET A
LITTLE WHILE, AND THE WORLD SEETH ME NO MORE; BUT YE SEE
ME: BECAUSE I LIVE, YE SHALL LIVE ALSO. AT THAT DAY YE SHALL
KNOW THAT I AM IN MY FATHER, AND YE IN ME, AND I IN YOU.

—JOHN 14:18-20

THE POWERS OF LOVE

GEORGE M. HORTON

It lifts the poor man from his cell
To fortune's bright alcove;
Its mighty sway few, few can tell,
Mid envious foes it conquers ill;
There's nothing half like love.

Ye weary strangers, void of rest,
Who late through life have strove,
Like the late bird which seeks its nest,
If you would hence in truth be blest,
Light on the bough of love.

The vagrant plebian, void of friends,
Constrain'd through wilds to rove,
On this his safety whole depends,
One faithful smile his trouble ends,
A smile of constant love.

Thus did a captured wretch complain,
Imploring heaven above,
Till one with sympathetic pain,
Flew to his arms and broke the chain,
And grief took flight from love.

Let clouds of danger rise and roar,
And hope's firm pillars move;
With storms behind and death before,
O grant me this, I crave no more,
There's nothing half like love.

When nature wakes soft pity's coo
The hawk deserts the dove,
Compassion melts the creature through,
With palpitations felt by few,
The wrecking throbs of love.

Let surly discord take its flight
From wedlock's peaceful grove,

While union breaks the arm of fight,
With darkness swallow'd up in light,
O what is there like love.[32]

CHARITY SUFFERETH LONG, AND IS KIND; CHARITY ENVIETH NOT;
CHARITY VAUNTETH NOT ITSELF, IS NOT PUFFED UP, DOTH NOT
BEHAVE ITSELF UNSEEMLY, SEEKETH NOT HER OWN, IS NOT EASILY
PROVOKED, THINKETH NO EVIL; REJOICETH NOT IN INIQUITY, BUT
REJOICETH IN THE TRUTH; BEARETH ALL THINGS, BELIEVETH ALL
THINGS, HOPETH ALL THINGS, ENDURETH ALL THINGS. CHARITY
NEVER FAILETH.

—1 CORINTHIANS 13:4-8

"Only God is able. It is faith in Him that we must redis-
cover. With this faith we can transform bleak and deso-
late valleys into sunlit paths of joy and bring new light
into the dark caverns of pessimism."

—DR. MARTIN LUTHER KING, JR.

MARIA STEWART

I believe, that for wise and holy purposes, best known to himself, He hath unloosed my tongue and put His word into my mouth,
in order to confound and put all those to shame that have rose up
against me. For He hath clothed my face with steel, and lined my
forehead with brass. He hath put His testimony within me, and

engraved His seal on my forehead. And with these weapons I have indeed set the fiends of earth and hell at defiance.

What if I am a woman; is not the God of ancient times the God of these modern days? Did He not raise up Deborah to be a mother and a judge in Israel? Did not Queen Esther save the lives of the Jews? And Mary Magdalene first declare the resurrection of Christ from the dead? Come, said the woman of Samaria, and see a man that hath told me all things that ever I did; is not this the Christ?

. . . If such women as are here described have once existed, be no longer astonished then, my brethren and friends, that God at this eventful period should raise up your own females to strive, by their example both in public and private, to assist those who are endeavoring to stop the strong current of prejudice that flows so profusely against us at present. No longer ridicule their efforts, it will be counted for sin. For God makes use of feeble means sometimes to bring about His most exalted purposes.

Why cannot a religious spirit animate us now? Why cannot we become divines and scholars? Although learning is somewhat requisite, yet recollect that those great apostles, Peter and James, were ignorant and unlearned. They were taken from the fishing boat and made fishers of men.

The dark clouds of ignorance are dispersing. The light of science is bursting forth. Knowledge is beginning to flow, nor will its moral influence be extinguished till its refulgent rays have spread over us from East to West, and from North to South. Thus far is this mighty work begun, but not as yet accomplished. Christians must awake from their slumbers. Religion must flourish among them before the Church will be built up in its purity, or immorality be suppressed.

Yet, notwithstanding your prospects are thus fair and bright, I am about to leave you, perhaps, never more to return. For I find it is no use for me as an individual to try to make myself useful among my color in this city. It was contempt for my moral and religious opinions in private that drove me thus before a public. Had experience more plainly shown me that it was the nature of man to crush his fellow, I should not have thought it so hard. Wherefore, my respected friends, let us no longer talk of prejudice, till prejudice becomes extinct at home. Let us no longer talk of opposition, till we cease to oppose our own. For while these evils exist, to talk is like giving breath to the air, and labor to the wind. Though wealth is far more highly prized than humble merit, yet none of these things move me. Having God for my friend and portion, what have I to fear?

. . . God has tried me as by fire. Well was I aware that if I contended boldly for His cause, I must suffer. Yet, I chose rather to suffer affliction with His people, than to enjoy the pleasures of sin for a season. And I believe that the glorious declaration was about to be made applicable to me, that was made to God's ancient covenant people by the prophet, comfort ye, comfort ye, My people: say unto her that her warfare is accomplished, and that her iniquities are pardoned.

I believe that a rich reward awaits me, if reflection. The bitterness of my soul has departed from those who endeavored to discourage and hinder me in my Christian progress; and I can now forgive and cheerfully pray for those who have despitefully used and persecuted me. Fare you well, farewell.[33]

THOU WILT KEEP THEM

EFFIE WALLER SMITH

Thou in perfect peace will keep them,
They whose minds on Thee are stayed;
Though the evil one may tempt them,
They shall still be unafraid.

Clouds may lower and darkness gather,
Billows furiously may roll;
Need we trouble when our Father
Speakest peace unto the soul.

Peace without one ray of terror,
Peace that comforts day by day;
Peace that passeth understanding,
May it keep our hearts alway![34]

THOU WILT KEEP HIM IN PERFECT PEACE, WHOSE MIND IS STAYED
ON THEE: BECAUSE HE TRUSTETH IN THEE.

—ISAIAH 26:3

IN THY SECRET PLACE

EFFIE WALLER SMITH

In Thy secret place, Most High,
Let us ever dwell;
Guarded by Thy watchful eye,
All shall e'er be well.

For when dwelling there, we know
That we shall abide
Underneath Thy wing's great shade,
Safely by Thy side.

With Thy wings then cover us;
They shall keep us warm,
And the weather chill and drear
Never can us harm.

Yea, when comes the raging storm,
Keep us still with Thee;
Round us put Thy mighty arms,
And we safe shall be.[35]

HE THAT DWELLETH IN THE SECRET PLACE OF THE MOST HIGH
SHALL ABIDE UNDER THE SHADOW OF THE ALMIGHTY. I WILL SAY
OF THE LORD, HE IS MY REFUGE AND MY FORTRESS: MY GOD; IN
HIM WILL I TRUST.

—PSALM 91:1-2

HIS ANSWER

CLARA ANN THOMPSON

He prayed for patience; Care and Sorrow came,
And dwelt with him, grim and unwelcome guests;
He felt their galling presence night and day;
And wondered if the Lord had heard him pray,
And why his life was filled with weariness.

He prayed again; and now he prayed for light;
The darkness parted, and the light shone in;
And lo! he saw the answer to his prayer—
His heart had learned, through weariness and care,
The patience, that he deemed he'd sought in vain.[36]

WE . . . REJOICE IN HOPE OF THE GLORY OF GOD. AND NOT ONLY SO, BUT WE GLORY IN TRIBULATIONS ALSO: KNOWING THAT TRIBULATION WORKETH PATIENCE; AND PATIENCE, EXPERIENCE; AND EXPERIENCE, HOPE: AND HOPE MAKETH NOT ASHAMED; BECAUSE THE LOVE OF GOD IS SHED ABROAD IN OUR HEARTS BY THE HOLY GHOST WHICH IS GIVEN UNTO US.

—ROMANS 5:2-5

LEAVE IT THERE

CHARLES A. TINDLEY

If the world from you withhold of its silver and its gold,
And you have to get along with meager fare,
Just remember, in His Word, how He feeds the little bird;
Take your burden to the Lord and leave it there.

Leave it there, leave it there,
Take your burden to the Lord and leave it there.
If you trust and never doubt, He will surely bring you out.
Take your burden to the Lord and leave it there.

If your body suffers pain and your health you can't regain,
And your soul is almost sinking in despair,
Jesus knows the pain you feel, He can save and He can heal;
Take your burden to the Lord and leave it there.

When your enemies assail and your heart begins to fail,
Don't forget that God in heaven answers prayer;
He will make a way for you and will lead you safely through.
Take your burden to the Lord and leave it there.

When your youthful days are gone and old age is stealing on,
And your body bends beneath the weight of care;
He will never leave you then, He'll go with you to the end.
Take your burden to the Lord and leave it there.[37]

A HERITAGE OF GLORY

SOJOURNER TRUTH

"SWEET is the virgin honey, though the wild bee store it in a reed; and bright the jewelled band that circleth an Ethiop's arm; pure are the grains of gold in the turbid stream of the Ganges; and fair the living flowers that spring from the dull cold sod. Wherefore, thou gentle student, bend thine ear to my speech, for I also am as thou art; our hearts can commune together: To meanest matters will I stoop, for mean is the lot of mortal; will rise to noblest themes, for the soul hath a heritage of glory."[38]

AS IT IS WRITTEN, EYE HATH NOT SEEN, NOR EAR HEARD, NEITHER
HAVE ENTERED INTO THE HEART OF MAN, THE THINGS WHICH GOD
HATH PREPARED FOR THEM THAT LOVE HIM.

—1 CORINTHIANS 2:9

STRENGTH

HE GIVETH POWER TO THE FAINT;
AND TO THEM THAT HAVE NO MIGHT
HE INCREASETH STRENGTH.

ISAIAH 40:29

Everybody should believe that they can be the best. Maybe they won't make number one, but if they don't believe in their own greatness, it's hard to expect anybody else to take a chance on them.

—AL GREEN[39]

The prayer that sparks revival begins long before the countryside seems to awaken from its slumber in sin. It starts when men fall on their knees and cry out to God. That's where true intimacy with God takes place and we begin the journey of being transformed into the image of Christ. And as men are transformed, the course of a nation can be changed.

—WELLINGTON BOONE

Life is not a spectator sport. . . . If you're going to spend your whole life in the grandstand just watching what goes on, in my opinion you're wasting your life.

—JACKIE ROBINSON[40]

If you don't have confidence, you'll always find a way not to win.

—CARL LEWIS[41]

FROM A NARRATIVE OF SOJOURNER TRUTH

When Sojourner had been at Northampton a few months, she attended another camp-meeting, at which she performed a very important part.

A party of wild young men, with no motive but that of entertaining themselves by annoying and injuring the feelings of others, had assembled at the meeting, hooting and yelling, and in various ways interrupting the services and causing much disturbance. Those who had the charge of the meeting, having tried their persuasive powers in vain, grew impatient and tried threatening.

The young men, considering themselves insulted, collected their friends, to the number of a hundred or more, dispersed themselves through the grounds, making the most frightful noises, and threatening to fire the tents. It was said the authorities of the meeting sat in grave consultation, decided to have the ringleaders arrested, and sent for the constable, to the great displeasure of some of the company, who were opposed to such an appeal to force and arms. Be that as it may, Sojourner, seeing great consternation depicted in every countenance, caught the contagion, and, ere she was aware, found herself quaking with fear.

Under the impulse of this sudden emotion, she fled to the most retired corner of a tent, and secreted herself behind a trunk, saying to herself, "I am the only colored person here, and on me, probably, their wicked mischief will fall first, and perhaps fatally." But feeling how great was her insecurity even there, as the very tent began to shake from its foundations, she began to soliloquize as follows:

"Shall I run away and hide from the Devil? Me, a servant of the living God? Have I not faith enough to go out and quell that mob, when I know it is written—'One shall chase a thousand, and two put ten thousand to flight'? I know there are not a thousand here; and I know I am a servant of the living God. I'll go to the rescue, and the Lord shall go with and protect me.

"Oh," said she, "I felt as if I had three hearts! and that they were so large, my body could hardly hold them!"

She now came forth from her hiding place, and invited several to go with her and see what they could do to still the raging of the moral elements. They declined, and considered her wild to think of it.

The meeting was in the open fields—the full moon shed its saddened light over all—and the woman who was that evening to address them was trembling on the preachers' stand. The noise and confusion were now terrific. Sojourner left the tent alone and unaided, and walking some thirty rods to the top of a small rise of ground, commenced to sing, in her most fervid manner, with all the strength of her most powerful voice, the hymn on the resurrection of Christ—

> It was early in the morning—it was early in the morning,
>
> Just at the break of day—
>
> When he rose—when he rose—when he rose,
>
> And went to heaven on a cloud.

All who have ever heard her sing this hymn will probably remember it as long as they remember her. The hymn, the tune, the style, are each too closely associated with to be easily separated from herself, and when sung in one of her most animated moods, in the open air, with the utmost strength of her most powerful voice, must have been truly thrilling.

As she commenced to sing, the young men made a rush towards her, and she was immediately encircled by a dense body of the rioters, many of them armed with sticks or clubs as their weapons of defence, if not of attack.

As the circle narrowed around her, she ceased singing, and after a short pause, inquired, in a gentle but firm tone, "Why do you come about me with clubs and sticks? I am not doing harm to anyone." "We aren't a going to hurt you, old woman; we came to hear you sing," cried many voices, simultaneously. "Sing to us, old woman," cries one. "Talk to us, old woman," says another. "Pray, old woman," says a third. "Tell us your experience," says a fourth. "You stand and smoke so near me, I cannot sing or talk," she answered.

"Stand back," said several authoritative voices, with not the most gentle or courteous accompaniments, raising their rude weapons in the air. The crowd suddenly gave back, the circle became larger, as many voices again called for singing, talking, or praying, backed by assurances that no one should be allowed to hurt her—the speakers declaring with an oath, that they would "knock down" any person who should offer her the least indignity.

She looked about her, and with her usual discrimination, said inwardly: "Here must be many young men in all this assemblage, bearing within them hearts susceptible of good impressions. I will speak to them." She did speak; they silently heard, and civilly asked her many questions. It seemed to her to be given her at the time to answer them with truth and wisdom beyond herself. Her speech had operated on the roused passions of the mob like oil on agitated waters; they were, as a whole, entirely subdued, and only clamored when she ceased to speak or sing. Those who stood in the background, after the circle was enlarged, cried out,

"Sing aloud, old woman, we can't hear." Those who held the scepter of power among them requested that she should make a pulpit of a neighboring wagon. She said, "If I do, they'll overthrow it." "No, they shan't—he who dares hurt you, we'll knock him down instantly, d--n him," cried the chiefs. "No we won't, no we won't, nobody shall hurt you," answered the many voices of the mob. They kindly assisted her to mount the wagon, from which she spoke and sung to them about an hour.[42]

ACCORDING TO MY EARNEST EXPECTATION AND MY HOPE, THAT IN
NOTHING I SHALL BE ASHAMED, BUT THAT WITH ALL BOLDNESS,
AS ALWAYS, SO NOW ALSO CHRIST SHALL BE MAGNIFIED IN MY
BODY, WHETHER IT BE BY LIFE, OR BY DEATH.

—PHILIPPIANS 1:20

EXTREMISTS FOR LOVE

DR. MARTIN LUTHER KING, JR.

More and more I feel that the people of ill will have used time much more effectively than have the people of good will. We will have to repent in this generation not merely for the hateful words and actions of the bad people but for the appalling silence of the good people. Human progress never rolls in on wheels of inevitability; it comes through the tireless efforts of men willing to be co-workers with God, and without this hard work, time itself becomes an ally of the forces of social stagnation. We must use time creatively, in the knowledge that the time is always ripe to do right. Now is the time to make real the promise of democracy and transform our pending national elegy into a creative psalm of brotherhood.

Was not Jesus an extremist for love: "Love your enemies, bless them that curse you, do good to them that hate you, and pray for them which despitefully use you, and persecute you." Was not

Amos an extremist for justice: "Let justice roll down like waters and righteousness like an ever-flowing stream." Was not Paul an extremist for the Christian gospel: "I bear in my body the marks of the Lord Jesus." Was not Martin Luther an extremist: "Here I stand; I cannot do otherwise, so help me God."

And John Bunyan: "I will stay in jail to the end of my days before I make a butchery of my conscience." And Abraham Lincoln: "This nation cannot survive half slave and half free." And Thomas Jefferson: "We hold these truths to be self-evident, that all men are created equal . . ." So the question is not whether we will be extremists, but what kind of extremists will we be.

Will we be extremists for hate or for love? Will we be extremists for the preservation of injustice or for the extension of justice? In that dramatic scene on Calvary's hill three men were crucified. We must never forget that all three were crucified for the same crime—the crime of extremism. Two were extremists for immorality, and thus fell below their environment. The other, Jesus Christ, was an extremist for love, truth and goodness, and thereby rose above his environment. Perhaps the South, the nation and the world are in dire need of creative extremists.[43]

THE FIRST OF ALL THE COMMANDMENTS IS, HEAR, O ISRAEL; THE LORD OUR GOD IS ONE LORD: AND THOU SHALT LOVE THE LORD THY GOD WITH ALL THY HEART, AND WITH ALL THY SOUL, AND WITH ALL THY MIND, AND WITH ALL THY STRENGTH: THIS IS THE FIRST COMMANDMENT. AND THE SECOND IS LIKE, NAMELY THIS, THOU SHALT LOVE THY NEIGHBOUR AS THYSELF. THERE IS NONE OTHER COMMANDMENT GREATER THAN THESE.

—MARK 12:29-31

HARRIET TUBMAN

"I can't die but once."

—HARRIET TUBMAN

Hail, oh hail, ye happy spirits,
Death no more shall make you fear,
Grief nor sorrow, pain nor anguish,
Shall no more distress you there.

Around Him are ten thousand angels,
Always ready to obey command;
Dey are always hovering round you,
Till you reach de heavenly land.

Jesus, Jesus will go wid you,
He will lead you to his throne;
He who died, has gone before you,
Trod de wine-press all alone.

He whose thunders shake creation,
He who bids de planets roll;
He who rides upon the tempest,
And whose scepter sways de whole.

> *Dark; and thorny is de pathway,*
> *Where de pilgrim makes his ways;*
> *But beyond dis vale of sorrow,*
> *Lie de fields of endless days.*[44]

> *I freed a thousand slaves. I could have freed a thousand*
> *more if only they knew they were slaves.*
>
> —HARRIET TUBMAN

UNCLE THOMAS ANDERSON

Uncle Thomas Anderson's conversion experience, as told by himself, December 24, 1854, when he was in his sixty-ninth year.

I was born a slave in Hanover County, Virginia, and being very much exposed in my boyhood—no one taking any interest in my welfare—I became very wicked, and remained so till I arrived at the age of nineteen, at which time I was singularly led to attend a religious meeting held by the Baptists (who was a very humble people at that time), when I was awakened to a sense of my condition from these words, dropped from a humble minister:

"The wicked have no hope beyond the grave, while the righteous have a hope beyond Jordan's cold stream; and after they have crossed Jordan they have gone home to a God of pity, to a God of compassion, to a God of sovereign mercy." These words took a deep hold on my wicked heart, and break up the great deep in my soul. And this prepare me to seek such a friend. And after searching a long season of time, the Friend of Sinners appear and fill my heart with love. He give me peace of soul and confidence of mind; then I could gladly tell this glorious Savior's mine. This destroyed all earthly fear, and prepare me to rest in hope. And then I could say, by sea or land, by day or night: "The Lord is ever mine!" Forty odd years I travel on in this way, and it now appears more precious than the first. And now I say:

> Come all who would live quiet here,
>
> This gracious Savior try;
>
> Lay down thy arms and earthly care,
>
> And you will find a Savior nigh!

Now, I would be glad for all the world to know that after I was awakened, as I have described, that love, in place of fear, fill my heart. Maybe I better say here that very often, when I goin' on in wickedness, something tell me this wicked, and I feel very bad. At that time I did not know that it was that good Spirit talking with me; yet I know all the time that I was doing wrong, 'cause I feel guilty, and that make me afraid.

But when I give all up to serve the Lord, He promise He help whenever I need Him. And soon after, He try my faith very strong. My master who owned me at that time having no knowledge of God or godliness, supposed my religion was all a fancy, and said he could and would whip it out of me. He took me up and tie me, and scourged me until feeling of flesh was almost gone. At length I fall before him and lift up my cries to Heaven, and ask my great Creator, "What have I done?" My master cursed me, and said: "Will you preach to me?" But I now feel glad that I could suffer patiently for my new Master. And my manner at that time take master's strength away; and before he left me he untie me and let me off. But in about three hours he come again, and threaten me with fresh scourging.

And though I was very weak from the beating I got, the Lord make me feel very strong, and this prepare me to answer: "You have whipped out all fear, and I am not afraid of you no more. You can take a gun and shoot me or kill me, as you please, and all for nothing; and that is all you can do: for I know I have a life you cannot touch, and the fear of you will not keep me from doing anything my new Master tells me to do.

"And if He let you take this poor bruised body of flesh, I feel it ain't worth much"; and I feel strength to say something like this: "Thy will, O God, be done and not mine!" After this my old master was conquered, and never whip me again, and left me in the hands of Jehovah. This give me confidence to talk to the white or the black folks, and tell what the Lord had done for my poor soul.[45]

TO KNOW HIM

JOHN JEA

COME, O thou Traveller unknown,
Whom still I hold, but cannot see!
My company before is gone,
And I am left alone with thee:
With thee all night I mean to stay,
And wrestle till the break of day.

I need not tell thee who I am;
My misery and sin declare:
Thyself hast call'd me by my name;

Look on thy hands, and read it there:
But who, I ask thee, who art thou?
Tell me thy Name, and tell me now.

In vain thou strugglest to get free,
I never will unloose my hold,
Art thou the Man that died for me?
The secret of thy love unfold:
Wrestling I will not let thee go,
Till I thy Name, thy Nature know.

Wilt thou not yet to me reveal
Thy new, unutterable Name?
Tell me, I still beseech thee, tell;
To know it now, resolv'd I am:
Wrestling I will not let thee go,
Till I thy Name, thy Nature know.

What though my shrinking flesh complain,
And murmur to contend so long?
I rise superior to my pain:
When I am weak, then I am strong:
And when my all of strength shall fail,
I shall with the God-man prevail.[46]

THE CONVERSION OF SOJOURNER TRUTH

We will now turn from the outward and temporal to the inward and spiritual life of our subject [Sojourner Truth]. It is ever both interesting and instructive to trace the exercises a human mind, through the trials and mysteries of life, and especially a naturally powerful mind, left as hers was almost entirely to its own workings, and the chance influences it met on its way; and especially to note its reception of that divine "light, that lighteth every man that cometh into the world."

We see, as knowledge dawns upon it, truth and error strangely commingled; here, a bright spot illuminated by truth—and there, one darkened and distorted by error; and the state of such a soul may be compared to a landscape at early dawn, where the sun is seen superbly gilding some objects, and causing others to send forth their lengthened, distorted, and sometimes hideous shadows.

Her mother, as we have already said, talked to her of God. From these conversations, her incipient mind drew the conclusion that God was "a great man"; greatly superior to other men in power; and being located "high in the sky," could see all that transpired on the earth. She believed He not only saw, but noted down all her actions in a great book, even as her master kept a record of whatever he wished not to forget. But she had no idea that God knew a thought of hers till she had uttered it aloud.

. . . Previous to these exercises of mind, she heard Jesus mentioned in reading or speaking, but had received from what she heard no impression that He was any other than an eminent man, like a Washington or a Lafayette. Now He appeared to her delighted mental vision as so mild, so good, and so every way lovely, and He loved her so much! And, how strange that He had always loved her, and she had never known it! And how great a blessing He conferred, in that He should stand between her and God! And God was no longer a terror and a dread to her.

She stopped not to argue the point, even in her own mind, whether He had reconciled her to God, or God to herself (though she thinks the former now), being but too happy that God was no longer to her as a consuming fire, and Jesus was "altogether lovely." Her heart was now full of joy and gladness, as it had been of terror, and at one time of despair. In the light of her great happiness, the world was clad in new beauty, the very air sparkled as with diamonds and was redolent of heaven. She contemplated the unapproachable barriers that existed between herself and the great of this world, as the world calls greatness, and made surprising comparisons between them, and the union existing between herself and Jesus—Jesus, the transcendently lovely as well as great and powerful; for so He appeared to her, though He seemed but human; and she watched for His bodily appearance feeling that she should know Him, if she saw Him; and when He came, she should go and dwell with Him, as with a dear friend.

. . . She commenced anew her labors, in the hope of yet being able to accumulate a sufficiency to make a little home for herself in her advancing age. With this stimulus before her, she toiled hard, working early and late, doing a great deal for a little money, and turning her hand to almost anything that promised good pay. Still, she did not prosper; and somehow, could not contrive to lay by a single dollar for a "rainy day."

When this had been the state of her affairs some time, she suddenly paused, and taking a retrospective view of what had passed, inquired within herself why it was that for all her unwearied labors she had nothing to show; why it was that others, with much less care and labor, could hoard up treasures for themselves and children? She became more and more convinced, as she reasoned, that everything she had undertaken in the city of New York had finally proved a failure; and where her hopes had been raised the highest, there she felt the failure had been the greatest, and the disappointment most severe.

After turning it in her mind for some time, she came to the conclusion that she had been taking part in a great drama, which was, in itself, but one great system of robbery and wrong. "Yes," she said, "the rich rob the poor, and the poor rob one another." True, she had not received labor from others, and stinted their pay, as she felt had been practised against her; but she had taken their work from them, which was their only means to get money, and was the same to them in the end. For instance, a gentleman where she lived would give her a half dollar to hire a poor man to clear the new-fallen snow from the steps and sidewalks. She would arise early and perform the labor herself, putting the money into her own pocket.

Her next decision was that she must leave the city; it was no place for her; yea, she felt called in spirit to leave it, and to travel east and lecture. She had never been further east than the city, neither had she any friends there of whom she had particular reason to expect anything; yet to her it was plain that her mission lay in the East, and that she would find friends there. She determined on leaving; but these determinations and convictions she kept close locked in her own breast, knowing that if her children and friends were aware of it, they would make such an ado about it as would render it very unpleasant, if not distressing to all parties.

Having made what preparations for leaving she deemed necessary—which was to put up a few articles of clothing in a pillow-case, all else being deemed an unnecessary encumbrance—about an hour before she left, she informed Mrs. Whiting, the woman of the house, where she was stopping, that her name was no longer Isabella, but SOJOURNER; and that she was going east. And to her inquiry, "What are you going east for?" her answer was, "The Spirit calls me there, and I must go."[47]

THE SPIRIT OF THE LORD GOD [IS] UPON ME; BECAUSE THE LORD HATH ANOINTED ME TO PREACH GOOD TIDINGS UNTO THE MEEK; HE HATH SENT ME TO BIND UP THE BROKENHEARTED, TO PROCLAIM LIBERTY TO THE CAPTIVES, AND THE OPENING OF THE PRISON TO [THEM THAT ARE] BOUND; TO PROCLAIM THE ACCEPT-ABLE YEAR OF THE LORD, AND THE DAY OF VENGEANCE OF OUR GOD; TO COMFORT ALL THAT MOURN; TO APPOINT UNTO THEM THAT MOURN IN ZION, TO GIVE UNTO THEM BEAUTY FOR ASHES, THE OIL OF JOY FOR MOURNING, THE GARMENT OF PRAISE FOR THE SPIRIT OF HEAVINESS; THAT THEY MIGHT BE CALLED TREES OF RIGHTEOUSNESS, THE PLANTING OF THE LORD, THAT HE MIGHT BE GLORIFIED.

—ISAIAH 61:1-3

WISDOM

IF ANY OF YOU LACK WISDOM,
LET HIM ASK OF GOD,
THAT GIVETH TO ALL MEN LIBERALLY,
AND UPBRAIDETH NOT; AND IT SHALL BE GIVEN HIM.

JAMES 1:5

Memories of our lives, of our works,
and our deeds will continue in others.

—ROSA PARKS

ON VIRTUE

PHYLLIS WHEATLEY

O THOU bright jewel, in my aim I strive
To comprehend thee. Thine own words declare
Wisdom is higher than a fool can reach.
I cease to wonder, and no more attempt
Thine height to explore, or fathom thy profound.
But O my soul, sink not into despair;
Virtue is near thee, and with gentle hand
Would now embrace thee—hovers o'er thine head.
Fain would the heaven-born soul with her converse,
Then seek, then court her for her promised bliss.
Auspicious queen! thine heavenly pinions spread,
And lead celestial Chastity along.
Lo! now her sacred retinue descends,
Arrayed in glory from the orbs above.
Attend me, Virtue, through my youthful years;
Oh, leave me not to the false joys of time,
But guide my steps to endless life and bliss.
Greatness, or Goodness, say what shall I call thee,
To give an higher appellation still:
Teach me a better strain, a nobler lay,
O thou, enthroned with cherubs in the realms of day.[48]

I COUNT ALL THINGS BUT LESS FOR THE EXCELLENCY OF THE
KNOWLEDGE OF CHRIST JESUS MY LORD . . . THAT I MAY WIN
CHRIST, AND BE FOUND IN HIM, NOT HAVING MINE OWN RIGHT-
EOUSNESS, WHICH IS OF THE LAW, BUT THAT WHICH IS THROUGH
THE FAITH OF CHRIST, THE RIGHTEOUSNESS WHICH IS OF GOD BY
FAITH: THAT I MAY KNOW HIM, AND THE POWER OF HIS RESURREC-
TION, AND THE FELLOWSHIP OF HIS SUFFERINGS, BEING MADE CON-
FORMABLE UNTO HIS DEATH.

—PHILIPPIANS 3:8-10

I'LL KEEP YOU SCRATCHING

SOJOURNER TRUTH

Previous to the war, Sojourner Truth held a series of meetings in northern Ohio. She sometimes made very strong points in the course of her speech, which she knew hit the apologist of slavery pretty hard. At the close of one of these meetings, a man came up to her and said, "Old woman, do you think that your talk about slavery does any good? Do you suppose people care what you say? Why," continued he, "I don't care any more for your talk than I do for the bite of a flea." "Perhaps not," she responded, "but, the Lord willing, I'll keep you scratching."[49]

A SONG OF JOY

JOHN QUINCY ADAMS

Great God of nations, now to Thee,
Our hymn of gratitude we raise;
That thou hast made this nation free,
We offer Thee our song of praise.

Thy name we bless, Almighty God,
For all the kindness Thou hast shown
To this fair land, by pilgrims trod—
This land we fondly call our own.

Here, freedom spreads its banner wide,
And casts its soft and hallowed ray:
Here, Thou our fathers' steps didst guide,
In safety, through their dangerous way.

We praise Thee, that the gospel light,
Through all our land, its radiance sheds,
Dispels the shades of error's night,
And heavenly blessings round us spreads.[50]

I have often thought that if I could do as I think, what a satisfaction it would be to me. What is there more desirable than wisdom? Nothing is more commendable, nothing more worthy of a great and illustrious man than mildness and clemency. A shameful flight from death is worse than any death. What is more disgraceful than inconstancy, levity, and fickleness? Nothing is more delightful than true glory. Nothing is more friendly to me than solitude. My country is much dearer to me than my life. No place ought to be more pleasing to you than your country. What is better in man than a sagacious and good mind? What can we call more wretched than folly? What is more pleasing than literary ease? Nothing is more inconstant than the common people. Nothing is more uncertain than the inclination of mankind. Nothing, believe me, is more handsome, nothing more beautiful, nothing more lovely, than virtue.

—JOHN QUINCY ADAMS[51]

YOUR OBEDIENCE IS COME ABROAD UNTO ALL MEN. I AM GLAD THEREFORE ON YOUR BEHALF: BUT YET I WOULD HAVE YOU WISE UNTO THAT WHICH IS GOOD, AND SIMPLE CONCERNING EVIL.

—ROMANS 16:19

WHOSO GIVES FREELY

JOSEPHINE DELPHINE HENDERSON HEARD

WHEN Jesus was leaving this sin-accursed land,
These words full of comfort he left with his band:
"Ye are not forsaken, my peace I will leave,
And whoso gives freely, shall freely receive!

"Your Father in heaven, so righteous and just,
Will comfort your hearts, if in Him ye trust;
If only on Jesus, His Son, ye believe;
Then ye who give freely, shall freely receive!

"On the just and the unjust descendeth the rain—
The fields all revived bring abundance of grain;
Give honor and glory and firmly believe,
That whoso gives freely, shall freely receive.

"Step out from your door on a bleak winter day—
Half-clad and half-starving, you meet on your way,
Someone who is begging for alms to relieve.
Think! whoso gives freely, shall freely receive!

"Perhaps but a penny dropped into a hat—
Yet the angel recording will take note of that.
Like the mite of the widow, whatever you give,
Much or little—give freely, you'll freely receive!

"There are often around us dear souls in distress,
Who are needing not money, but kind words to bless—
Their lives seem so weary—a word will relieve;
Let's give to them freely, they'll gladly receive!

"When finished our course in this vale here below,
When Christ shall the robe and the crown bestow
On those, who were faithful and quick to believe:
Who gave Him their service shall freely receive!"[52]

GO RATHER TO THE LOST SHEEP OF THE HOUSE OF ISRAEL. AND AS
YE GO, PREACH, SAYING, THE KINGDOM OF HEAVEN IS AT HAND.
HEAL THE SICK, CLEANSE THE LEPERS, RAISE THE DEAD, CAST OUT
DEVILS: FREELY YE HAVE RECEIVED, FREELY GIVE.

—MATTHEW 10:6-8

DO YOU THINK?

JOSEPHINE DELPIHNE HENDERSON HEARD

Do you think, when you plan for tomorrow,
That the morrow you may not see,
That long ere the dawn of the morrow's morn,
You may be in eternity?

Do you tread in the footsteps of Jesus,
In the darkness as well as the light?
Should the death angel come, to summon you
Home—
Say, would it be glory, or night?[53]

THE DAY OF THE LORD WILL COME AS A THIEF IN THE NIGHT; IN
THE WHICH THE HEAVENS SHALL PASS AWAY WITH A GREAT NOISE,
AND THE ELEMENTS SHALL MELT WITH FERVENT HEAT, THE EARTH
ALSO AND THE WORKS THAT ARE THEREIN SHALL BE BURNED UP.

—2 PETER 3:10

FORGIVENESS

BE YE THEREFORE MERCIFUL,
AS YOUR FATHER ALSO IS MERCIFUL.
JUDGE NOT, AND YE SHALL NOT BE JUDGED:
CONDEMN NOT, AND YE SHALL NOT BE CONDEMNED:
FORGIVE, AND YE SHALL BE FORGIVEN.

LUKE 6:36-37

If you are carrying strong feelings about something that happened in your past, they may hinder your ability to live in the present.

—LES BROWN[54]

We cannot be facile and say bygones will be bygones, because they will not be bygones and will return to haunt us. True reconciliation is never cheap, for it is based on forgiveness which is costly. Forgiveness in turn depends on repentance, which has to be based on an acknowledgement of what was done wrong, and therefore on disclosure of the truth. You cannot forgive what you do not know.

—DESMOND TUTU[55]

Most Christians ignore the true difference between forgiveness and repentance. To ask forgiveness is to say, "I'm sorry." But since the effects are rarely lasting in those instances, I wonder if it really means, "I'm sorry...that I was caught." To repent for something literally means "to turn away from." Men of God need to turn their backs upon everything unsanctified so that they can become all that they are capable of being. It is much the same with reconciling and restoring. To reconcile is to make amends in the eyes of God and man; to be restored is to walk in those amendments and fulfill the call that the Lord has placed upon our lives.

—T. D. JAKES[56]

PERSEVERANCE

HE THAT SHALL ENDURE UNTO THE END,
THE SAME SHALL BE SAVED.

MARK 13:13

For, we are a people who have been through hell and lived to sing about it. And that means that we know that our God is a God of justice and power, and that the gates of hell cannot prevail against His will.

—ALAN KEYES[57]

It is a dangerous thing to ask why someone else has been given more. It is humbling—and indeed healthy—to ask why you have been given so much.

—CONDOLEEZZA RICE[58]

If you train hard, you'll not only be hard, you'll be hard to beat.

—HERSCHEL WALKER[59]

Set your goals high and don't stop until you get there.

—BO JACKSON[60]

ON BEING BROUGHT FROM AFRICA TO AMERICA

PHYLLIS WHEATLEY

IT WAS mercy brought me from my pagan land,
Taught my benighted soul to understand
That there's a God—that there's a Saviour too:
Once I redemption neither sought nor knew.
Some view our sable race with scornful eye—
"Their color is a diabolic dye."
Remember, Christians, Negroes black as Cain
May be refined, and join the angelic train.[61]

WE KNOW THAT ALL THINGS WORK TOGETHER FOR GOOD TO THEM
THAT LOVE GOD, TO THEM WHO ARE THE CALLED ACCORDING TO
HIS PURPOSE.

—ROMANS 8:28

STAND BY ME

CHARLES TINDLEY

When the storms of life are raging,
Stand by me (stand by me);
When the storms of life are raging,
Stand by me (stand by me);

When the world is tossing me
Like a ship upon the sea
Thou Who rulest wind and water,
Stand by me (stand by me).

In the midst of tribulation,
Stand by me (stand by me);
In the midst of tribulation,
Stand by me (stand by me);
When the hosts of hell assail,
And my strength begins to fail,
Thou Who never lost a battle,
Stand by me (stand by me).

In the midst of faults and failures,
Stand by me (stand by me);
In the midst of faults and failures,
Stand by me (stand by me);
When I do the best I can,
And my friends misunderstand,
Thou Who knowest all about me,
Stand by me (stand by me).

In the midst of persecution,
Stand by me (stand by me);

In the midst of persecution,
Stand by me (stand by me);
When my foes in battle array
Undertake to stop my way,
Thou Who savèd Paul and Silas,
Stand by me (stand by me).

When I'm growing old and feeble,
Stand by me (stand by me);
When I'm growing old and feeble,
Stand by me (stand by me);
When my life becomes a burden,
And I'm nearing chilly Jordan,
O Thou "Lily of the Valley,"
Stand by me (stand by me). [62]

THE WATCHER

CLARA ANN THOMPSON

A faithful watcher sits alone,
And waits to see the Old Year die;
And sober are the thoughts that come,
As silently the hours slip by—
The dear Old Year is almost gone;
Full soon I'll say a sad "Farewell";

I ask myself, what good I've done;
What deeds of love have I to tell?

Have I been patient, kind, and just,
Forgiving, loving, faithful, true,
During the year that dies tonight,
And yields his scepter to the New?

Perchance, I have more patient been,
More faithful, than in years now gone,
But, ah, I've greater heights to win,
Trusting the Grace that leads me on.

And this, my pray'r tonight shall be,
While glad bells chime: "The guest is here."
Oh, gracious Father, guide Thou me,
And keep Thy children through this year!

The watcher ends his simple pray'r
And lo! a deep peace fills his soul;
He fearless greets the glad New Year,
For God, the Father, has control.[63]

In the dispensation of the fullness of times he might gather together in one all things in Christ, both which are in heaven, and which are on earth; even in him: In whom also we have obtained an inheritance, being predestinated according to the purpose of him who worketh all things after the counsel of his own will: That we should be to the praise of his glory, who first trusted in Christ.

—Ephesians 1:10-12

He Leadeth Me

Effie Waller Smith

When cloudless and sunlit skies o'erspread
Their azure robes above my head,
When 'bout my pathway flowers grow
Richer than the Orient's blooms,
Than the Orient's sweet perfumes:
'Tis pleasant then His will to know.

When winds are still and when the air
Is filled with music sweet and rare,
Far sweeter than the sirens knew
Far sweeter strains than ever came
From Orpheus' harp wild beasts to tame:
'Tis pleasant then His will to do.

But, oh, when dark and threat'ning clouds

My once fair sunlit sky enshrouds,
And when bright flowers I do not see,
When winds like maddened billows roar,
When music charms my ears no more,
You ask how it's then with me?

How is it then my pathway's strewn
With sharpened stone and prickly thorn,
Darkness about me, daylight gone?
It all I cannot understand,
But with my hand in His own hand
I say: "Dear Father, lead me on."[64]

I WILL NEVER LEAVE THEE, NOR FORSAKE THEE.

—HEBREWS 13:5

OLD ELIZABETH

In the following narrative of "Old Elizabeth," taken mainly from her own lips in her 97th year, her simple language has been adhered to as strictly as was consistent with perspicuity and propriety.

I was born in Maryland in the year 1766. My parents were slaves. Both my father and mother were religious people, and belonged to the Methodist Society. It was my father's practice to read in the Bible aloud to his children every Sabbath morning. At these sessions, when I was but five years old, I often felt the overshadowing of the Lord's Spirit, without at all understanding what it meant; and these incomes and influences continued to attend me until I was eleven years old, particularly when I was alone, by which I was preserved from doing anything that I thought was wrong.

In the eleventh year of my age, my master sent me to another farm, several miles from my parents, brothers, and sisters, which was a great trouble to me. At last I grew so lonely and sad I thought I should die, if I did not see my mother. I asked the overseer if I might go, but being positively denied, I concluded to go without his knowledge. When I reached home my mother was away. I set off and walked twenty miles before I found her. I staid with her for several days, and we returned together.

Next day I was sent back to my new place, which renewed my sorrow. At parting, my mother told me that I had, "nobody in the wide world to look to but God." These words fell upon my heart with ponderous weight, and seemed to add to my grief. I went back repeating as I went, "none but God in the wide world." On reaching the farm, I found the overseer was displeased at me for going with-out his liberty. He tied me with a rope, and gave me some stripes of which I carried the marks for weeks.

After this time, finding as my mother said, I had none in the world to look to but God, I betook myself to prayer, and in every lonely place I found an altar. I mourned sore like a dove and chat-tered forth my sorrow, moaning in the corners of the field, and under the fences.

I continued in this state for about six months, feeling as though my head were waters, and I could do nothing but weep. I lost my appetite, and not being able to take enough food to sustain nature, I became so weak I had but little strength to work; still I was required to do all my duty. One evening, after the duties of the day were ended, I thought I could not live over the night, so threw myself on a bench, expecting to die, and without being prepared to meet my Maker; and my spirit cried within me, must I die in this state, and be banished from Thy presence forever? I own I am a sinner in Thy sight, and not fit to live where Thou art. Still it was my fervent desire that the Lord would pardon me.

Just at this season, I saw with my spiritual eye, an awful gulf of misery. As I thought I was about to plunge into it, I heard a voice saying, "Rise up and pray," which strengthened me. I fell on my knees and prayed the best I could the Lord's prayer. Knowing no more to say, I halted, but continued on my knees. My spirit was then taught to pray, "Lord, have mercy on me—Christ save me." Immediately there appeared a director, clothed in white raiment. I thought He took me by the hand and said, "Come with Me." He led me down a long journey to a fiery gulf, and left me standing upon the brink of this awful pit. I began to scream for mercy, thinking I was about to be plunged to the belly of hell, and believed I should sink to endless ruin. Although I prayed and wrestled with all my might, it seemed in vain. Still, I felt all the while that I was sustained by some invisible power.

At this solemn moment, I thought I saw a hand from which hung, as it were, a silver hair, and a voice told me that all the hope I had of being saved was no more than a hair; still, pray, and it will be sufficient. I then renewed my struggle, crying for mercy and salvation, until I found that every cry raised me higher and higher, and my head was quite above the fiery pillars. Then I thought I was permitted to look straight forward, and saw the Saviour standing with His hand stretched out to receive me. An indescribably glorious light was in Him, and He said, "peace, peace, come unto Me."

At this moment I felt that my sins were forgiven me, and the time of my deliverance was at hand. I sprang forward and fell at His feet, giving Him all the thanks and highest praises, crying, "Thou hast redeemed me—Thou hast redeemed me to thyself." I felt filled with light and love. At this moment I thought my former guide took me again by the hand and led me upward, till I came to the celestial world and to Heaven's door, which I saw was open, and while I stood there, a power surrounded me which drew me in, and I saw millions of glorified spirits in white robes. After I had this view, I thought I heard a voice saying, "Art thou willing to be saved?" I said, "Yes, Lord." Again I was asked, "Art thou willing to be saved in My way?" I stood speechless until He asked me again, "Art thou willing to be saved in My way?" Then I heard a whispering voice say, "If thou art not saved in the Lord's way, thou canst not be saved at all"; at which I exclaimed, "Yes, Lord, in Thy own way."

Immediately a light fell upon my head, and I was filled with light, and I was shown the world lying in wickedness, and was told I must go there, and call the people to repentance, for the day of the Lord was at hand; and this message was as a heavy yoke upon me, so that I wept bitterly at the thought of what I should have to pass through. While I wept, I heard a voice say, "Weep not, some will laugh at thee, some will scoff at thee, and the dogs will bark at thee, but while thou doest My will, I will be with thee to the ends of the earth."

I was at this time not yet thirteen years old. The next day, when I had come to myself, I felt like a new creature in Christ, and all my desire was to see the Saviour.

I lived in a place where there was no preaching, and no religious instruction; but every day I went out amongst the haystacks, where the presence of the Lord overshadowed me, and I was filled with sweetness and joy, and was as a vessel filled with holy oil. In this way I continued for about a year; many times while my hands were at my work, my spirit was carried away to spiritual things.[65]

He that dwelleth in the secret place of the most High
shall abide under the shadow of the Almighty.

—Psalm 91:1

The Young African

A.V. Griswold

The young African, whose arrival in this city in company with the Rev. Dr. Savage, was noticed in the Witness and Advocate of the 20th October, 1843, is now numbered with the dead. His father is king of the Barbo tribe, and he and his people are still living in the lowest depths of heathenism.

"Wana Hobah" (his native name) was taken into the mission school of the American Protestant Episcopal Church at Cape Palmas in 1836, being then about ten years of age, and but little elevated in intellectual condition above the beasts of the forest.

He was the fifth of the fifteen native youths who, for several years past, have been supported at the mission stations in Africa by the scholars and teachers of Grace Church Sunday school in this city, and by their request he was named A. V. Griswold.

His improvement at the Mission school was very satisfactory, particularly in view of the fact that a foreign language was to be acquired before he could advance a step in other studies. We found him, after only a few years' instruction by our missionaries in Africa, well versed in the scriptures, and the doctrines and services of our church, in grammar, geography, arithmetic, and writing, and no stranger to the study of philosophy and astronomy.

The following extract from the notice referred to will show the impression produced on those who saw him soon after his arrival in Boston, in October 1843:

"He reads fluently and without embarrassment, and whoever had the privilege and pleasure of witnessing his interesting examination, which took place in Grace Church Sunday school, on Sunday morning, could not but thank God for such an evidence of the blessed nature of the missionary work, and of the faithfulness of our missionaries in Africa. Especially must they have been gratified with his ready and appropriate answers to the questions put to him by the Rev. Mr. C., in reference to the leading doctrines of the Christian religion."

The object which Dr. Savage had in view in bringing him to America was that he might learn the art of printing, then return to his native land and take his station at the missionary press.

During his residence in this city, he was in the family of Mr. and Mrs. Perkins, who had Griswold under their care when in Africa, two or three years since; and was also a regular attendant at the Sunday school of Grace Church. He was kindly taken into the printing-office of T. R. Marvin, Esq., and every person connected with the establishment manifested a deep and lively interest in his welfare. The following extract of a letter written by Griswold to his father, dated October 31st, is interesting evidence of the state of his mind, after his first month's residence in this city:

"I have very good friends here, I am living with Mr. Perkins. I am now learning to print, so as to come home and print books for our countrymen. I have seen the mighty works of the Lord. I have seen water hard as stone, and burns like fire. Witch never touch me. I am well. The Lord is with me, so you and all the old men ought to throw away your grudges and serve God, because He only is able to save your souls from eternal punishment of hell.

"The leaves of the trees are falling off now, and as these leaves are falling, so we all shall fall. O what a greater punishment it must be to them that hear the word of God and do not do it; if we do not love God for all the things He has done for us, and above all, for sending His only begotten Son, Jesus Christ, to die for us."

After his death, the following was found among his few books and papers, being the hasty draft of a letter written by him during the visit of Dr. Savage here in April 1844, and addressed to a young friend in the Mission school at Cape Palmas:

"Dear Friend: I am very glad to hear that you are all well. So we all are here. But how is my poor old father and mother and all my friends?

"I would advise you, my dear young friends of the Mission schools, to keep up as great a strife and earnestness in religion, as if you knew yourselves to be in a state of nature, and were seeking conversion.

"Persons are advised, under conviction, to be earnest and violent for the kingdom of Heaven, but when they have attained to conversion, they ought not to be the less watchful, laborious and earnest in the whole work of religion, but the more so, for they are under infinite greater obligations.

"For want of this, many persons, in a few months after their conversion, have begun to lose their sweet and lively sense of spiritual things, and to grow dark, and have 'pierced themselves through with many sorrows.' Whereas, if you do as the apostle did, your path shall be 'as the shining light, which shineth more and more unto the perfect day.'"

A manuscript was also found among his papers, which gave good evidence of his familiar acquaintance with, and regard for, the *Book of Common Prayer*. Several pages were written in the Barbo language, comprising the opening sentences, exhortation, and the Lord's Prayer.

Being intelligent and quick to learn, his improvement was rapid, and he bid fair soon to accomplish the object for which he came to this country. But the wise and overruling providence of God has ordered otherwise. After having passed through one of our severest winters with almost entire exemption from disease, during which he was seldom absent from his accustomed employment, and when all danger from the severity of our climate seemed to be over, he was attacked, on Sunday, May 5th, 1844, with inflammation of the lungs. Although the disease was developed with considerable severity, still his case was not considered hopeless until within a few hours of his death, which happened on the twelfth day. About noon, on Thursday, the 16th, a change took place for the worse, and notwithstanding the most energetic treatment, he continued to sink until a little before midnight, when he quietly breathed his last. The writer of this cannot but bear testimony to the untiring efforts of Dr. H. to alleviate the sufferings of the deceased, and to the unceasing and patient labors of Mr. and Mrs. Perkins, who watched over him by day and by night.

In reviewing Griswold's course of life during his seven or eight months' residence among us, it is pleasant to be able to state that his Bible was his most constant companion. Always on returning from his daily avocation at evening, he was in the habit of seating himself at the table with his Bible and dictionary before him. He would read carefully; look up the definition of difficult words; and when not able to understand in this way, make inquiry of others. He was regular in his private devotions, and frequently when Mr. Perkins had occasion to go into his chamber, he has found him on his knees, praying to his Father in secret.

His acquaintance with the Old and New Testaments was often brought out in the Sunday school. When questions of a general nature were asked, and there was any hesitation or delay in answering, an appeal to Griswold was seldom made in vain. His prompt and pertinent manner of replying will not soon be forgotten. During his sickness, and when the trying hour of death drew near, he seemed to find great comfort and consolation in prayer, and in the promises of God's Word which he had so constantly and diligently studied.[66]

WHAT TO DO?

LUCY LARCOM

"If the world seems cold to you,
Kindle fires to warm it!
Let their comfort hide from view
Winters that deform it.
Hearts as frozen as your own
To that radiance gather;
You will soon forget to moan,
'Ah, the cheerless weather!'

"If the world's a wilderness,
Go build houses in it!
Will it help your loneliness
On the winds to din it?
Raise a hut, however slight;
Weeds and brambles smother;
And to roof and meal invite
Some forlorner brother.

"If the world's a vale of tears,
Smile till rainbows span it!
Breathe the love that life endears,
Clear from clouds to fan it.
Of your gladness lend a gleam
Unto souls that shiver;
Show them how dark Sorrow's stream
Blends with Hope's bright river."

How far you go in life depends on your being tender with
the young, compassionate with the aged, sympathetic
with the striving and tolerant of the weak and strong.
Because someday in your life you will have been all of
these.

—GEORGE WASHINGTON CARVER

RT. REVEREND RICHARD ALLEN

JOANNA P. MOORE

OUR Richard Allen in his early youth,
Sought out and found the way of light and truth;
His heart with holy impulse was stirred,
And boldly forth he went to preach the word.

Sometimes he had not even a resting-place—

Footsore and weary, still he cried free grace;
And yet in pastures green the shepherd fed,
And by the cooling stream was often led.

Year after year is born and glides away;
Generations rise and flourish and decay;
Flowers bud and blossom, fade and fall,
But eternal truth outlives them all.

And so a hundred years have passed away,
Since the immortal Allen's natal day;
And where he sleeps the sun's departing ray
Long lingers, o'er that hallowed heap of clay.

He came of humble parentage to earth;
A slave was he of meek and lowly birth;
A bondsman dared not even raise his voice,
Nor o'er his young, his darling child rejoice.

But God his promises, has ever kept,
And the foul stigma from this land is swept—
At last the slavish chains forever broke,
And falls at last the bondman's galling yoke.

As they march on you hear their steady tread,
With Allen's banner waving overhead;
The cause of Christ to distant islands borne—
O, flourish till the resurrection morn![67]

GOD HATH CHOSEN THE FOOLISH THINGS OF THE WORLD
TO CONFOUND THE WISE; AND GOD HATH CHOSEN THE WEAK
THINGS OF THE WORLD TO CONFOUND THE THINGS
WHICH ARE MIGHTY.

—1 CORINTHIANS 1:27

THEREFORE, MY BELOVED BRETHREN, BE YE STEDFAST,
UNMOVEABLE, ALWAYS ABOUNDING IN THE WORK OF THE LORD,
FORASMUCH AS YE KNOW THAT YOUR LABOUR IS
NOT IN VAIN IN THE LORD.

—1 CORINTHIANS 5:58

OUR NEED FOR CHRIST

HE SAID UNTO ME, MY GRACE IS SUFFICIENT FOR THEE:
FOR MY STRENGTH IS MADE PERFECT IN WEAKNESS.
MOST GLADLY THEREFORE WILL I RATHER GLORY IN
MY INFIRMITIES, THAT THE POWER OF CHRIST
MAY REST UPON ME.

2 CORINTHIANS 12:9

Sanctification is the normal experience of every Christian. God set us apart for himself the moment Christ redeemed us. In fact, anyone who isn't sanctified isn't saved. And every believer is a saint, a "holy one." So don't let anyone tell you that sanctification is a spiritual experience that we must seek after salvation or a holy status only achieved by the elite.

—ANTHONY EVANS[68]

Let me tell you something. If you have never made the decision to follow Jesus Christ whatever the cost . . . .Don't be surprised if you don't see much answered prayer.

—ANTHONY EVANS[69]

I met a man named Jesus, and I had an exchange with Him. I gave Him my sorrows, He gave me His joy; I gave Him my confusion, He gave me His peace; I gave Him my despair, He gave me His hope; I gave Him my hatred, He gave me His love; I gave Him my torn life, He gave me His purpose.

—OTIS MOSS[70]

While man said that we should be slaves, God said we should be free. Now we are free. What is our duty? To serve God with all the heart that He may bless us while we live here on earth. The man who does not fear God has not much hope for eternal life.

JOHN QUINCY ADAMS[71]

THE ONE FAMILY

JOHN QUINCY ADAMS

God of love, before Thee now,
Help us all in love to bow;
As the dews on Hermon fall,
May Thy blessing rest on all.

Let it soften every breast,
Hush ungentle thoughts to rest,
Till we feel ourselves to be
Children of one family;

Children who can look above,
For a heavenly Father's love;
Who shall meet, life journey past,
In that Father's house at last.

But, while thankfully we meet,

> *Thus, around Thy mercy-seat,*
> *Yet, one humble, earnest plea,*
> *Father, we would bring to Thee.*
>
> *Far across the ocean's wave*
> *Brethren, sisters too, we have;*
> *But they have not heard of Thee:*
> *Wilt Thou not their Father be?*
>
> *Let them hear the Shepherd's voice,*
> *And beneath His care rejoice;*
> *And together let us come*
> *To the fold: "There yet is room."*[72]

A BRAND PLUCKED
FROM THE FIRE

JULIA A. J. FOOTE

The Christian who does not believe in salvation from all sin in this life, cannot have a constant, complete peace. The evil of the heart will rise up and give trouble. But let all such remember the words of Paul: "I am crucified with Christ; nevertheless, I live; yet not I, but Christ liveth in me; and the life which I now live in the flesh, I live by faith of the Son of God, who loved me, and gave himself for me." "Ask, and ye shall receive." The blood of Jesus will not only purge your conscience from the guilt of sin, and from dead works, but it will destroy the very root of sin that is in the heart, by faith, so that you may serve the living God in the beauty of holiness.

My earnest desire is that many—especially of my own race—may be led to believe and enter into rest, "For we which have believed do enter into rest"—sweet soul rest.

I was converted when fifteen years old. It was on a Sunday evening at a quarterly meeting. The minister preached from the text: "And they sung as it were a new song before the throne, and before the four beasts, and the elders: and no man could learn that song but the hundred and forty and four thousand, which were redeemed from the earth" (Revelation 14:3).

As the minister dwelt with great force and power on the first clause of the text, I beheld my lost condition as I never had done before.

Something within me kept saying, "Such a sinner as you are can never sing that new song." No tongue can tell the agony I suffered. I fell to the floor, unconscious, and was carried home. Several remained with me all night, singing and praying. I did not recognize anyone, but seemed to be walking in the dark, followed by someone who kept saying, "Such a sinner as you are can never sing that new song." Every converted man and woman can imagine what my feelings were. I thought God was driving me on to hell. In great terror I cried: "Lord, have mercy on me, a poor sinner!"

The voice which had been crying in my ears ceased at once, and a ray of light flashed across my eyes, accompanied by a sound of far distant singing; the light grew brighter and brighter, and the singing more distinct, and soon I caught the words: "This is the new song—redeemed, redeemed!" I at once sprang from the bed where I had been lying for twenty hours, without meat or drink, and commenced singing: "Redeemed! Redeemed! Glory! Glory!" Such joy and peace as filled my heart, when I felt that I was redeemed and could sing the new song. Thus was I wonderfully saved from eternal burning.

. . . Though my gifts were but small, I could not be shaken by what man might think or say. I continued day by day, month after month, to walk in the light as He is in the light, having fellowship with the Trinity and those aged saints. The blood of Jesus Christ cleansed me from all sin, and enabled me to rejoice in persecution. Bless the Lord, O my soul, for this wonderful salvation, that snatched me as a brand from the burning, even me, a poor, ignorant girl!

And will He not do for all what He did for me? Yes, yes; God is no respecter of persons. Jesus' blood will wash away all your sin and make you whiter than snow.[73]

STORY OF THE CHRIST-CHILD

EFFIE WALLER SMITH

Would the muses me inspire,
I today would tell to you
Story old of the Christ-child,
Dear old story, sweet and true.

How at night the lowly shepherds
Watched their flocks on Judea's hills,
While the night-wind's music mingled
With the music of the rills.

I would tell you of the tidings
Which were borne that night to them,
"Peace on earth, good will to men,
Christ is born in Bethlehem."

I would tell you how those shepherds,
In that country far away,
Came to where within a manger
The sweet little Christ-child lay.

I would tell you how the wise men,
From the western plains afar,
Guided were into Bethlehem
By a bright and wondrous star.

I would tell you how they worshipped
Him, the infant Jesus dear,
How they gave Him costly presents,
Gold and frankincense and myrrh.

I would tell you all about it,
All about this story old,
Of the Christ-child in the manger,
Though I know it's oft been told.

But the gift to paint word-pictures
Suitable for such a birth;
Suitable for One so holy;
For the Saviour of the earth,

Is denied me. I can only,
I can only tell you where
You can find this beauteous story—
In the Bible. Read it there![74]

VIRGINIA W. BROUGHTON

Although Virginia was interested in Bible band work, she had no dream of doing missionary work, for she was teaching at a lucrative salary, and fully engaged in her home and school duties. About this time Virginia's beloved mother, the joy of her heart, was called to her home beyond the skies. This blow came like a clap of thunder in a clear sky—the deepest sorrow Virginia had ever known up to that time.

The whole world seemed lone and drear to Virginia, and her greatest comfort came from the hope of soon departing this life and joining her mother in the blessed homeland of the soul. Virginia's health was poor and she felt so confident she would soon die. She resigned her position in the school and moved off to another city, where she hoped her children would be cared for, should she die.

Conditions and circumstances were so unsatisfactory she did not remain long in her adopted city, but soon returned to her former home. In the spring of 1887 Virginia had a very serious illness; her life was despaired of; she had selected her burial robes, and made such other preparations as she deemed necessary, and with intense longing to depart she lay on her bed waiting on the Lord for the expected summons.

Husband, children, and all other earthly ties and possessions were given up. By and by the Lord manifestly came, but not as she expected, to bear her ransomed spirit home, but she was overshadowed with the veritable presence of God, and made to understand thoroughly and clearly in language spoken to the soul, that God was not ready for her then, but He had a work for her to do. That marvelous experience was accompanied with renewed strength of body that continued to increase from that moment until she was able to leave her bed.

Virginia's physical weakness, at that time, prohibited her from witnessing a great baptizing that she desired greatly to see, but she was given another rich spiritual blessing that more than compensated her for failing to see the baptizing. She was privileged to hear sweet heavenly music that is unlawful for man to utter, and she quietly rested, sweetly rejoicing in the Lord, as a babe lulled to rest in its mother's arms. In time her strength increased and she came to her normal condition of health. The following song was at once given her, suggestive of many of her experiences, and also as one of the ways God would direct her in her work.

> "How firm a foundation, ye saints of the Lord,
> Is laid for your faith in His excellent Word;
> What more can He say, than to you He hath said,
> You, who with Jesus, for refuge hath fled?"

This song, through all these twenty years, has not only been an inspiration for service, but its truths have been verified in the varied experiences we herein relate.

Virginia gladly began her work again in the Bible class taught by Mrs. M. Ehlers, the stationed missionary in her home city. The first meeting she attended after her recovery was one of great joy to her; she was so full of joy she spoke twice in that meeting, and then and there won friends to the Lord's cause that have ever since proved faithful allies of hers in the great work of missions where unto God had called her.

As God hath declared in Isaiah 54:17, "No weapon that is formed against thee shall prosper; and every tongue that shall rise against thee in judgment thou shalt condemn." We found it true; glory be to God! Virginia was tried to the uttermost, and persecuted with cruel hatred for no other cause than her contention for holiness of heart, and uprightness of daily deportment.

A general awakening in the study of the Bible followed these great meetings. Bible texts were repeated around the firesides and at the dining room tables as well as in Sunday school and other religious meetings. A general reform was evidently going on toward the development of the women and the betterment of the home and church life of the people. Women were giving up the vile habits of beer drinking and snuff-dipping, and using their little mites thus saved in getting our Christian literature and contributing to our missionary and educational work.

At the beginning of her missionary work she was comfortably situated in her own home, with other possessions that brought her a small income. Her husband was not a professor of religion at the beginning of her missionary career, and naturally was greatly opposed to her frequently going from home. One day he asked her, "When is this business going to stop?"

She replied, "I don't know; but I belong to God first, and you next; so you two must settle it." Truly God inspired that answer. She took herself absolutely out of the management of the affair and accepted the humble position of an obedient servant. God verily did settle the question. He convinced the husband fully that He had called his wife to a special service and to hinder her would mean death to him. Of course there was no alternative; the husband, after a desperate struggle with the world, the flesh and the devil, yielded to God, and made an open profession of faith in Jesus and joined the church militant. This husband has ever since been helpful in attending to much of the business connected with Virginia's missionary work these twenty years.[75]

PETER RANDOLPH

Having briefly given the history of the overseers, I will now give my own, and how I, a slave, learned to read and write. Edloe owned eighty-one slaves, and among them all, only myself could either read or write.

When I was a child, my mother used to tell me to look to Jesus, and that He who protected the widow and fatherless would take care of me also. At that time, my ideas of Jesus were the same as those of the other slaves. I thought He would talk with me, if I wished it, and give me what I asked for. Being very sickly, my greatest wish was to live with Christ in Heaven, and so I used to go into the woods and lie upon my back, and pray that He would come and take me to himself—really expecting to see Him with my bodily eyes.

I was then between ten and eleven years old, and I continued to look for Him until I began to feel very sorry that He would not come and talk with me; and then I felt that I was the worst little boy that ever lived, and that was the reason Jesus would not talk to me. I felt so [upset] about it I wanted to die, and thought it would be just in God to kill me, and I prayed that He would kill me, for I did not want to live to sin against Him anymore. I felt so for many days and nights.

At last, I gave myself up to the Lord, to do what He would with me, for I was a great sinner. I began to see the offended justice of God. O, my readers, the anguish of my heart! I thought the whole world was on me, and I must die and be lost. In the midst of my troubles, I felt that if God would have mercy on me, I should never sin again. When I had come to this, I felt my guilt give way, and thought that I was a new being.

Now, instead of looking with my real eyes to see my Savior, I felt Him in me, and I was happy. The eyes of my mind were open, and I saw things as I never did before. With my mind's eye, I could see my Redeemer hanging upon the Cross for me.

I wanted all the other slaves to see Him thus, and feel as happy as I did. I used to talk to others, and tell them of the friend they would have in Jesus, and show them by my experience how I was brought to Christ, and felt His love within my heart—and love it was, in God's adapting himself to my capacity.

After receiving this revelation from the Lord, I became impressed that I was called of God to preach to the other slaves. I labored under this impression for seven years, but then I could not read the Bible, and I thought I could never preach unless I learned to read the Bible, but I had no one to teach me how to read.

A friend showed me the letters, and how to spell words of three letters. Then I continued, until I got so as to read the Bible—the great book of God—the source of all knowledge. It was my great desire to read easily this book. I thought it was written by the Almighty himself. I loved this book, and prayed over it and labored until I could read it.

I used to go to the church to hear the white preacher. When I heard him read his text, I would read mine when I got home. This is the way, my readers, I learned to read the Word of God when I was a slave. Thus did I labor eleven years under the impression that I was called to preach the gospel of Jesus Christ, the ever-blessed God.[76]

BLESSED IS THE MAN THAT WALKETH NOT IN THE COUNSEL OF THE UNGODLY, NOR STANDETH IN THE WAY OF SINNERS, NOR SITTETH IN THE SEAT OF THE SCORNFUL. BUT HIS DELIGHT IS IN THE LAW OF THE LORD; AND IN HIS LAW DOTH HE MEDITATE DAY AND NIGHT. AND HE SHALL BE LIKE A TREE PLANTED BY THE RIVERS OF WATER, THAT BRINGETH FORTH HIS FRUIT IN HIS SEASON; HIS LEAF ALSO SHALL NOT WITHER; AND WHATSOEVER HE DOETH SHALL PROSPER.

—PSALM 1:1-3

THOMAS L. JOHNSON

Those only who are acquainted with Mr. Johnson know the elasticity of his heart; how, unmindful of self, it throbs for Africa, the land of his forefathers, and that in loving tenderness it encircles every tribe, however degraded, in that vast continent.

Ever since receiving his first freedom, the liberty of his soul, through simply trusting his blessed Jesus, he longed to be the bearer of the glad tidings of salvation to his benighted countrymen; and no sooner had he gained his second freedom, that of his person, secured by the capture of Richmond, and overthrow of the Confederate government, than we find him diligently striving to secure the education necessary to the fulfillment of his long-cherished hopes; and although his path was strewn with difficulties, and for a time he seemed to make but little progress, yet by prayer and faith they were all surmounted.

We have the most unbounded confidence in Mr. Johnson, and earnestly pray God to bless and prosper him wherever he may be called to labour. It is now seventeen or eighteen years since we first met him as the Pastor of Providence Baptist Church, Chicago,

Illinois, beloved by his own people and respected by all.

He frequently spoke of Africa and his longing to go there, and once, when visiting him in a time of sickness, he said: "Oh, if God would only let me go to Africa and preach one sermon, I would be willing to die"; and this in a tone of such intense earnestness that we saw it to be of the Lord, who has proved how He can "fulfill the desire of them that fear Him," even "exceeding abundantly above all we ask or think."

For Mr. Johnson has not only laboured himself in Africa, but succeeded in planting a mission where Jesus was unknown, which still flourishes; and he is now an instrument, we believe, in the hand of an omnipotent God, to awaken the interest and enlist the sympathy of many others who shall carry the glorious Gospel to the dark hearts and homes of poor Africa, which seems to have borne the Cross as well as the curse for so many ages.

How shall we answer to the King in the day of His appearing, if we should withhold our sympathy, prayers, and money? Are we not responsible for the discipling of all nations? May a perusal of the following pages, which prove "all things are possible to him that believeth," lead to a deeper consecration, and a coveting of the privilege of a share in "Africa for Jesus," so that sower and reaper may rejoice together; for "all the promises of God are yea and amen in Christ Jesus."[77]

TWENTY-EIGHT YEARS A SLAVE

THOMAS L. JOHNSON

The first time I got five cents I went to a bookstore and asked for a copybook. I had made up my mind what to say if the bookseller should ask me who I wanted it for. However, he did not question me. I went home and commenced to teach myself how to write, or to learn from this book.

The letters were alphabetically arranged. I got on nicely, but another difficulty presented itself—I could not spell. I purchased a spelling book, kept it in my pocket, and every opportunity I would look into it. But there were so many words I could not understand.

At night, when the young master would be getting his lessons, I would select some word I wanted to know how to spell, and say, "Mos Carroll, I'll bet you can't spell 'looking glass.'" He would at once spell it. I would exclaim, "Lor's o'er me, Mos Carroll, you can spell it nice." Then I would go out and spell it over and over again. I knew that if I once got it into my head they could never get it out.

This young man was always willing to answer my questions; but sometimes he would ask why I wanted to know, and I would say, "I want to see how far you are." I carefully felt my way, knowing that, as a rule, all slaveholders objected to educated Negroes. In the course of time young Mr. Brent became very kind and free with me, and would often read to me portions of his lessons.

If I liked it and wanted to hear it again, I would say, "Lor's o'er me, Mos Carrol, read that again," which he often did. In this way each week I added a little to my small store of knowledge about this great world in which I lived.

But the door to freedom seemed as much closed as ever. There was a large map of the United States hanging on the wall in the dining room, and each day, as I attended to my cleaning, I would stop a few minutes and look at the map. In the course of time, I learned to spell nearly all the cities along the R. W. route from Richmond to Boston. Often I wondered whether I would ever see these cities, where all were free.

During all this time I was thinking more or less about seeking religion. Some of the slaves sang so much about "heaven," and "home," and "rest," and "freedom," and seemed so happy, that I often longed to be able to join them. The home beyond, where there was "perfect rest," and freedom, and peace, where there would be no slavery, was almost daily before me.

But how to get religion was what perplexed me; yet I felt it was essential to my happiness both here and hereafter. See how the heathen grope in the dark after God, and the dark heart turns towards Him. When I afterwards went to Africa I found the condition of plantation Negroes (in many instances) was but little better than that of the heathen in Africa. "How shall they hear without a preacher?" (Romans 10:14). Dear Christian reader, will not you do something to send the Gospel to them?

Hardly a day passed without someone of my own long-oppressed people being led to the whipping post, and there lashed most unmercifully. Every auction day many were sold away to Georgia, or some other of the far-off Southern states, and often they could be seen in companies, handcuffed, on their way to the Southern markets, doomed, doomed to perpetual slavery. "Oh," I would think, "I must seek religion!" In the year 1857 there was a great revival in America.

Many of the coloured people said the Judgment day was coming. Everywhere you could hear of great meetings and of thousands of souls being converted. There were many large tobacco factories in Richmond, working thousands of slaves, and I daily heard of many converts in these factories. First one and then another of my friends would set out to "seek religion."

At last I resolved, if I lived a thousand years, I would not stop seeking until I found peace; but the thought of meeting that old serpent, the devil, was chilling and repulsive to me. I often listened to the converts telling their experience, and I heard some say (as I remarked before) that, when they set out, the devil set out with them; that, while seeking, they would "fast and pray"; that the devil would do all he could to turn them back. I thought they had seen him with their natural eyes, and that I must also see him.

Above all things this troubled me the most, yet I made up my mind that I must meet him if I wanted religion. Then I thought I must in some way renovate myself; that, to be acceptable to God, I must fit myself. With this fixed upon my mind, on Wednesday, the 1st of June, 1857, I set out to "seek religion."

As night came on, my only thought was that I would meet the devil. I feared to go to bed, so sat out in the porch. Night after night I would sit there, and nod awhile, then awake in fear, looking round to see if the devil was near. If a cat came upon the wall, I feared it was the devil; if I heard a rat, I thought it was the devil; and thus I went on from night to night. During the day I did not speak to anyone. I had always been lively and cheerful; but now, looking as I did, the master wanted to know what was the matter, and he talked of sending me to Georgia.

I made up my mind, wherever I went, not to stop seeking until I found peace. I knew that God was stronger than the devil and the master. Hence I asked Him, "Please don't let master sell me to Georgia." After about two weeks, having fasted all I could some days, on others taking a hearty meal, and having lost so much rest night after night, I got at last into a state I cannot describe. I can only say it was a living death. When night came on, for fear of meeting the devil, I would wish for day; and when day came, I would regret that I had been such a coward during the night. I thought that, when I arrived at a state of not being afraid, God would meet me and take me by the hand, and show me some wonderful sight. At last it seemed to me I could not stand it any longer.

After nearly three weeks, I met a coloured man on the street, named Stephney Brown. He was a Christian, and quite an intelligent man. He explained to me the simple Gospel. He told me to go to God, and say: "Lord, have mercy upon me, a hell-deserving sinner, for Jesus' sake; set me out Your way and not my way, for Jesus' sake." "But," said he, "you must have faith.

"Now this is faith: If you came to see me, and asked me for a drink of water, you would expect and believe that I would give it to you. So you must ask God for Jesus' sake to have mercy upon you, a hell-deserving sinner. If you die as you are, you will go to hell, but you must ask pardon for Jesus' sake. He cannot deny you if you ask for Jesus' sake."

"For Jesus' sake" seemed to enter into my soul. "Have mercy upon me, a hell-deserving sinner, for Jesus' sake," rang through my heart all the way home, and I began to understand the finished work of my blessed Jesus as I never had before.

As soon as my work was done for that night, and all was quiet, I resolved that, if I lived for a thousand years, I would never stop praying "for Jesus' sake." I went into the dining room, fell down upon my knees, and said: "O Lord, have mercy upon me, a hell-deserving sinner, for Jesus' sake."

Then I became very happy. I got up and went into the porch. Everything appeared to be different to me. The very stars in the heaven seemed brighter, and I was feeling brighter and so very happy. I did not see any great sights, but there was an inward rejoicing. I had not done anything—I could not do anything—to merit this any more than the thief upon the Cross, but my blessed Jesus had done it all; there was nothing for me to do.

In the matter of salvation, all that God requires of us is to acknowledge with repentance our sins and receive with gratitude His salvation. The blood of Jesus had been accepted as the full atonement for the sin of the sinner. Oh, how many weary hearts and wasted lives there are today through failing to recognize this important truth.

The Blessed Christ has atoned for my sin, and all I have to do is to accept God's pardon, and eternal life. The Lord Jesus was now not one whom I had merely heard about, but He was my blessed Jesus—just as much mine as if there was no person besides myself in the world.[78]

THEREFORE IF ANY MAN BE IN CHRIST, HE IS A NEW CREATURE: OLD THINGS ARE PASSED AWAY; BEHOLD, ALL THINGS ARE BECOME NEW.

—2 CORINTHIANS 5:17

FREDERICK DOUGLASS

Previously to my contemplation of the anti-slavery movement and its probable results, my mind had been seriously awakened to the subject of religion. I was not more than thirteen years old, when in my loneliness and destitution I longed for someone to whom I could go, as to a father and protector. The preaching of a white Methodist minister, named Hanson, was the means of causing me to feel that in God I had such a friend. He thought that all men,

great and small, bond and free, were sinners in the sight of God:
that they were by nature rebels against His government; and that
they must repent of their sins, and be reconciled to God through
Christ.

I cannot say that I had a very distinct notion of what was
required of me, but one thing I did know well: I was wretched and
had no means of making myself otherwise. I consulted a good colored man named Charles Lawson, and in tones of holy affection he
told me to pray, and to "cast all my care upon God." This I sought to
do; and though for weeks I was a poor, broken-hearted mourner,
traveling through doubts and fears, I finally found my burden light-
ened and my heart relieved.

I loved all mankind, slaveholders not excepted, though I
abhorred slavery more than ever. I saw the world in a new light, and
my great concern was to have everybody converted. My desire to
learn increased, and especially did I want a thorough acquaintance
with the contents of the Bible. I have gathered scattered pages of the
Bible from the filthy street-gutters, and washed and dried them, that
in moments of leisure I might get a word or two of wisdom from
them.

While thus religiously seeking knowledge, I became acquainted with a good old colored man named Lawson. This man not only
prayed three times a day, but he prayed as he walked through the
streets, at his work, on his dray—everywhere. His life was a life of
prayer, and his words when he spoke to anyone, were about a better
world.

Uncle Lawson lived near Master Hugh's house, and becoming
deeply attached to him, I went often with him to prayer meeting,
and spent much of my leisure time with him on Sunday. The old
man could read a little, and I was a great help to him in making out
the hard words, for I was a better reader than he. I could teach him

"the letter," but he could teach me "the spirit," and refreshing times we had together in singing and praying.

These meetings went on for a long time without the knowledge of Master Hugh or my mistress. Both knew, however, that I had become religious, and seemed to respect my conscientious piety. My mistress was still a professor of religion and belonged to class. Her leader was no less a person than Rev. Beverly Waugh, the presiding elder, and afterwards one of the bishops of the Methodist Episcopal Church.

In view of the cares and anxieties incident to the life she was leading, and especially in view of the separation from religious associations to which she was subjected, my mistress had, as I have before stated, become lukewarm, and needed to be looked up by her leader. This often brought Mr. Waugh to our house, and gave me an opportunity to hear him exhort and pray.

But my chief instructor in religious matters was Uncle Lawson. He was my spiritual father and I loved him intensely and was at his house every chance I could get. This pleasure, however, was not long unquestioned. Master Hugh became averse to our intimacy and threatened to whip me if I ever went there again. I now felt myself persecuted by a wicked man, and I would go. The good old man had told me that the "Lord had a great work for me to do," and I must prepare to do it; that he had been shown that I must preach the Gospel. His words made a very deep impression upon me, and I verily felt that some such work was before me, though I could not see how I could ever engage in its performance. "The good Lord will bring it to pass in His own good time," he said, and that I must go on reading and studying the scriptures.

This advice and these suggestions were not without their influence on my character and destiny. He fanned my already intense love of knowledge into a flame by assuring me that I was to be a useful man in the world. When I would say to him, "How can these things be and what can I do?" his simple reply was, "Trust in the Lord." When I would tell him, "I am a slave, and a slave for life; how can I do anything?" he would quietly answer, "The Lord can make you free, my dear; all things are possible with Him; only have faith in God. 'Ask, and it shall be given you.' If you want liberty, ask the Lord for it in FAITH, and He will give it to you."

Thus assured and thus cheered on under the inspiration of hope, I worked and prayed with a light heart, believing that my life was under the guidance of a wisdom higher than my own. With all other blessings sought at the mercy seat, I always prayed that God would, of His great mercy and in His own good time, deliver me from my bondage.[79]

IF THE SON THEREFORE SHALL MAKE YOU FREE, YE SHALL BE FREE INDEED.

—JOHN 8:36

THANKSGIVING

ENTER INTO HIS GATES WITH THANKSGIVING,
AND INTO HIS COURTS WITH PRAISE:
BE THANKFUL UNTO HIM, AND BLESS HIS NAME.

PSALM 100:4

As soon as healing takes place,
go out and heal someone else.

—Maya Angelou

Continual Blessing

Andrae Crouch

God says in His Word that if we are faithful over a few, that He will make us ruler over many. That's when God can trust you, when you know from where your help comes. It doesn't come from the hills, it comes from God. My help comes from the Lord. It is nothing that we can put our hands on; it's a supernatural God thing when we can be trusted just to do what He has commanded us to do.

Nobody's perfect, but we do have a perfect foundation. If we do mess up, we don't run away from the altar, we run TO the altar, saying "God, I praise you for that, for this" and "God, I messed up."

If you make yourself available, and if you are striving, He won't do anything else but bless you. And the blessings are sometimes not what we think. He will overwhelm with things you don't even know about, with things that you've even forgotten were on your heart, and that you had asked Him about. You'll say, "Wow, God, You didn't forget about that!"

I'm overwhelmed that God just continually blesses. Since I've been pastor of the church [Christ Memorial Church in Los Angeles], I've had four forms of cancer and God has healed me each time. I wouldn't want to wake up in the morning without saying thank you for another day.[80]

WHOSO OFFERETH PRAISE GLORIFIETH ME: AND TO HIM THAT
ORDERETH HIS CONVERSATION AWRIGHT, I WILL SHOW
THE SALVATION OF GOD.

—PSALM 50:23

*Not only could I not do anything wrong from their point
of view . . . . They pulled it off so that I had that sense of
confidence, but they always reminded me that it could
have turned out differently, that I was fortunate, that
God blessed me to give me these opportunities, that you
shouldn't take them for granted, and that not everybody
had them.*

—CONDOLEEZZA RICE[81]

THE EMPTY TOMB

CLARA ANN THOMPSON

Calv'ry's tragedy is ended;
They have laid Him in the tomb,
And with jealous care, His enemies have sealed it;
But they cannot keep Him there,
For an earthquake rends the air,
And an angel rolls away the stone that closed it.
None are there to greet the Savior,
As He leaves the open tomb,
All forgotten are the promises He gave them;

And the women wend their way
To the tomb, ere it is day;
Not in faith, for death's sad emblems bring
they with them.

Oh, the darkness of that morning,
When they stood before His tomb,
With the spices and the ointments to anoint Him.
And I hear sad Mary say:
"They have taken Him away,
And I know not, and I know not where
they've laid Him."

Oh, ye ones of faithless doubting!
Know ye not what Jesus said,
While in life, His toil to you was freely given?
Now ye stand, with hearts of woe
While your bitter tears doth flow,
Knowing not your Lord and Savior has arisen.

Then the Savior speaks to Mary,
And at first, she knows Him not,
For her eyes are darkened by her doubts and sadness;
Then, He speaks to her again,
Gently calls her by her name,
And she greets her risen Lord with wondrous gladness.

Often in the Christians' struggle,
When the battle rages sore,
And on ev'ry side the bitter foes assail them,
E'en like her, they sadly say:
"They have taken Him away,
And I know not, and I know not where
they've laid Him."

And, like her, with bitter weeping,
As they face the empty tomb,
All His promises and wondrous deeds forgotten,
If they'd turn, they'd find Him near,
With such loving words of cheer,
That they'd know 'twas doubt, that made
them feel forsaken.[82]

NOW UPON THE FIRST DAY OF THE WEEK, VERY EARLY IN THE
MORNING, THEY CAME UNTO THE SEPULCHRE, BRINGING THE
SPICES WHICH THEY HAD PREPARED, AND CERTAIN OTHERS WITH
THEM. AND THEY FOUND THE STONE ROLLED AWAY FROM THE
SEPULCHRE. AND THEY ENTERED IN, AND FOUND NOT THE BODY
OF THE LORD JESUS. AND IT CAME TO PASS, AS THEY WERE MUCH
PERPLEXED THEREABOUT, BEHOLD, TWO MEN STOOD BY THEM IN
SHINING GARMENTS: AND AS THEY WERE AFRAID, AND BOWED
DOWN THEIR FACES TO THE EARTH, THEY SAID UNTO THEM, WHY
SEEK YE THE LIVING AMONG THE DEAD? HE IS NOT HERE, BUT IS
RISEN.

—LUKE 24:1-6

IN MEMORIAM (FREDERICK DOUGLASS)

H. CORDELIA RAY

One whose majestic presence ever here,
Was as an inspiration held so dear,
Will greet us nevermore upon the earth.
The funeral bells have rung; there was no dearth
Of sorrow as the solemn cortege passed;
But ours is a grief that will outlast
The civic splendor. Say, among all men,
Who was this hero that they buried then,
With saddest plaint and sorrow-stricken face?

Ay! 'Twas a princely leader of his race!
And for a leader well equipped was he;
Nature had given him most regally
E'en of her choicest gifts. What matter then
That he in chains was held, what matter when
He could uplift himself to noblest heights.

E'en with his native greatness, neither slights
Nor wrongs could harm him; and a solemn wrath
Burned in his soul. He well saw duty's path;
His days heroic purposes did know,
And could he then his chosen work forego?

Born to a fate most wretched, most forlorn!
A slave! Alas! Of benefits all shorn
Upon his entrance into life, what lot
More destitute of hope! Yet e'en that blot
Could not suffice to dim the glowing page
He leaves to History; for he could wage
Against oppression's deadliest blows a war
That knew no ending, until nevermore
Should any man be called a bondman. Ay!
Such was a conflict for which one could die.

Panting for freedom early, he did dare
To throw aside his shackles, for the air

Of slavery is poison unto men
Molded as Douglass was; they suffer, then
Manhood asserts itself; they are too brave,
Such souls as his, to die content a slave.
So being free, one path alone he trod,
To bring to liberty—sweet boon from God—
His deeply injured race; his tireless zeal
Was consecrated to the bondman's weal.

He thought of children sobbing round the knees
Of hopeless mothers, where the summer breeze
Blew o'er the dank savannas. What of woe
In their sad story that he did not know!
He was a valiant leader in a cause
Than none less noble, though the nation's laws
Did seem to spurn it; and his matchless speech
To Britain's sea-girt island shores did reach.
Our Cicero, and yet our warrior knight,
Striving to show mankind might is not right!

He saw the slave uplifted from the dust,
A freeman! Loyal to the sacred trust
He gave himself in youth, with voice and pen,
He had been to the end. And now again
The grandest efforts of that brain and heart
In ev'ry human sorrow bore a part.

His regnant intellect, his dignity,
Did make him honored among all to be;
And public trusts his country gladly gave
Unto this princely leader, born a slave!

Shall the race falter in its courage now
That the great chief is fallen? Shall it bow
Tamely to aught of injury? Ah, nay!
For daring souls are needed e'en to-day.
Let his example be a shining light,
Leading through duty's paths to some far height
Of undreamed victory. All honored be
The silv'ry head of him we no more see!
Children unborn will venerate his name,
And History keep spotless his fair fame.

The Romans wove bright leafy crowns for those
Who saved a life in battle with their foes;
And shall not we as rare a chaplet weave
To that great master-soul for whom we grieve?
Yea! Since not always on the battlefield
Are the best vict'ries won; for they who yield
Themselves to conquer in a losing cause,
Because 'tis right in God's eternal laws,
Do noblest battle; therefore fitly we
Upon their brows a victor's crown would see.

Yes! Our great chief has fallen as might fall
Some veteran warrior, answering the call
Of duty. With the old serenity,
His heart still strung with tender sympathy,
He passed beyond our ken; he'll come no more
To give us stately greeting as of yore.
We cannot fail to miss him. When we stand
In sudden helplessness, as through the land
Rings echo of some wrong he could not brook,
Then vainly for our leader will we look.

But courage! No great influence can die.
While he is doing grander work on high,
Shall not his deeds an inspiration be
To us left in life's struggle? May not we
Do aught to emulate him whom we mourn?
We are a people now, no more forlorn
And hopeless. We must gather courage then,
Rememb'ring that he stood man among men.
So let us give, now he has journeyed hence,
To our great chieftain's memory, reverence![83]

THE JUST MAN WALKETH IN HIS INTEGRITY: HIS CHILDREN ARE
BLESSED AFTER HIM.

—PROVERBS 20:7

FREDERICK DOUGLASS

THEODORE TILTON

"I knew the noblest giants of my day,
And he was of them—strong amid the strong:
But gentle too: for though he suffered wrong,
Yet the wrong-doer never heard him say,
'Thee also do I hate.' . . .

"A lover's lay—
No dirge—no doleful requiem song—
Is what I owe him; for I loved him long;
As dearly as a younger brother may.

"Proud is the happy grief with which I sing;
For, O my Country, in the paths of men
There never walked a grander man than he!
He was a peer of princes—yea, a king!
Crowned in the shambles and the prison-pen!
The noblest Slave that ever God set free!"[84]

THE STEPS OF A GOOD MAN ARE ORDERED BY THE LORD: AND HE
DELIGHTETH IN HIS WAY. THOUGH HE FALL, HE SHALL NOT BE
UTTERLY CAST DOWN: FOR THE LORD UPHOLDETH HIM WITH HIS
HAND. I HAVE BEEN YOUNG, AND NOW AM OLD; YET HAVE I NOT
SEEN THE RIGHTEOUS FORSAKEN, NOR HIS SEED BEGGING BREAD.
HE IS EVER MERCIFUL, AND LENDETH; AND HIS SEED IS BLESSED.

—PSALM 37:23-26

MARY F. MCCRAY

Our subject was greatly urged to seek the Lord. She went forward and soon found that she was a lost sinner without the blood of Jesus to wash away all her sins.

They would work hard all day in the cornfields and nearly every night would go two or three miles from home to attend meetings. Many were converted every night. She was somewhat discouraged because she was so slow to believe. Her cousin fell under the mighty power of God and was happily converted, coming through shouting and praising God, and commenced at once to preach to the people, telling them to flee from the wrath to come.

She said to our subject to believe and she would be converted. This encouraged her to go on. She was trying to get converted, shouting like her cousin, but the Dear Lord did not come to her in that way. She did reason with the devil for some time, who told her that if she did not shout she would not have religion. She had a terrible struggle to get over that.

After that terrible struggle about getting converted shouting, her faith was greatly increased, and while she was praying one day she was wonderfully blessed. She told her cousin how she felt. Her cousin told her that she had religion. She said, "Oh, no, I am just getting in a good way." She did not understand the scheme of the devil, so she was defeated and had to do her work all over again. But the Holy Spirit still strove with her.

The meetings were still going on with increased power. She attended nearly every night. The old people encouraged her, and then she began to take part in speaking and praying. By so doing the same blessing came to her again, but she was not satisfied. She went on in that state quite a long time. Finally one night she went to bed and fell into a dream, or trance, she did not know which.

However, a man came to her while she was in that vision. She was trying to cross a clear stream of water. The man she believed to be a white man. He threw a narrow board in the middle of the stream of water, and there was also a broad board in the stream. The man told her to make her choice. She stepped on the narrow one and went across. As soon as she was across he showed her a beautiful place and told her it was Heaven. She saw her cousin there and she was with all the angels. They were all just alike. She turned to come back, when she heard a voice saying: "You have just as much religion as those who shout."

After that she woke up. She felt very strange and told her aunt about the vision. Her aunt said that she would get through all right. In a short time afterwards she received the witness of the Holy Spirit that her sins were all forgiven. She was then a happy girl. She knew that her sins were all washed away by the blood of Jesus. She could sing this song:

"Oh! happy day, that fixed my choice,
On Thee, my Savior and my God;
Well may this glowing heart rejoice,
And tell its rapture all abroad.

Happy day! Happy day!
When Jesus washed my sins away.
He taught me how to watch and pray,
And live rejoicing every day,
Happy day! Happy day!
When Jesus washed my sins away."

The meeting spread from one plantation to another, and many of the poor slaves' hearts were made to rejoice, for the Lord Jesus visited them, notwithstanding they were treated only as cattle and horses. Thanks be unto the Lord God of Heaven, who did look down upon them in their helpless condition in tender mercy.[85]

*I*NTEGRITY

⎯⎯⎯◉⎯⎯⎯

*"There may be terrible consequences for being good.
There may be suffering, there may be death, there may
be deprivation. But we still have the choice. We can spit
it all in the eye, [or] we can stand strong for what we
know to be right. And in death we would vindicate the
liberty that God has put in our hearts: the liberty to
choose His way."*

ALAN KEYES, HILLSDALE, MICHIGAN, FEBRUARY 7, 2004

It all goes so fast, and character makes the difference when it's close.

—JESSE OWENS[86]

We've laid down these basic principles for the kids: integrity, service, initiative, discipline, and faith. Without these five pillars, you're not going to be successful.

—DAVID ROBINSON[87]

God doesn't call the equipped; He equips the called.

—WELLINGTON BOONE

We thought the way up is up. But with God, the way up is down.

—WELLINGTON BOONE

Character is doing the right thing when nobody's looking. There are too many people who think that the only thing that's right is to get by, and the only thing that's wrong is to get caught.

—J.C. WATTS

I was always someone who led by actions, not words.

—Barry Sanders[88]

FAITH OF OUR FATHERS

J.C. WATTS

Let me be blunt. The first step we can take toward restoring our nation is for each of us to recognize that we, as individual citizens, have all too often drifted with the cultural tide that has brought us to this unhappy place. We have not, for example, reached out to the many lonely and directionless kids in our communities, or even to our own kids. We have left the television on in order to entertain and babysit our children. We have succumbed to the easy role of trumpeting our beliefs at the expense of listening to others. We have fallen for the sound bite mentality, which is a poor substitute for personal reflection and responsible action. And as a nation, we have refused to accept the fact that we are now reaping what almost every one of us has sown. Make no mistake. We should not be surprised that some of our children are killing each other in our schools and on our streets. We should not be shocked that many of our children have no sense of purpose, and feel hopeless and empty even in this era of unprecedented plenty. We should not be surprised that, in the absence of the faith of our fathers, our children have adopted bizarre creeds, beliefs, and practices. We truly are reaping what we have sown. And it is a very bitter harvest. We have all played a role in getting us here, and we all have a role to play in taking us home.[89]

THEN THOSE WHO FEARED THE LORD SPOKE TO ONE ANOTHER,
AND THE LORD GAVE ATTENTION AND HEARD IT, AND A BOOK OF
REMEMBRANCE WAS WRITTEN BEFORE HIM FOR THOSE WHO FEAR
THE LORD AND WHO ESTEEM HIS NAME.

—MALACHI 3:16

*The American Dream is about becoming the best you
can be. It's not about your bank account, the kind of car
you drive, or the brand of clothes you wear. It's about
using your gifts and abilities to be all that God meant for
you to be.*

—GOP NATIONAL CONVENTION SPEECH, AUGUST 13, 1996

*You may not accomplish every goal you set — no one
does — but what really matters is having goals and
going after them wholeheartedly. In the end, it is the
person you become, not the things you achieve, that is
most important.*

—LES BROWN[90]

NOTHING BETWEEN

CHARLES TINDLEY

Nothing between my soul and my Savior,
Naught of this world's delusive dream;
I have renounced all sinful pleasure;
Jesus is mine, there's nothing between.

Nothing between, like worldly pleasure;
Habits of life, though harmless they seem;
Must not my heart from Him ever sever;
He is my all, there's nothing between.

Nothing between, like pride or station;
Self or friends shall not intervene;
Though it may cost me much tribulation,
I am resolved, there's nothing between.

Nothing between, e'en many hard trials,
Though the whole world against me convene;
Watching with prayer and much self denial,
I'll triumph at last, there's nothing between.[91]

WRITTEN FOR THE OCCASION OF THE GARRISON CENTENARY

H. CORDELIA RAY, DECEMBER 10, 1905

Some names there are that win the best applause
Of noble souls; then whose shall more than thine
All honored be? Thou heardst the Voice Divine
Tell thee to gird thyself in Freedom's cause,
And cam'st in life's first bloom. No laggard laws
Could quench thy zeal until no slave should pine
In galling chains, caged in the free sunshine.
Till all the shackles fell, thou wouldst not pause.
So to thee who hast climbed heroic heights,
And led the way to where chaste Justice reigns,
An anthem—tears and gratitude and praise,
Its swelling chords—uprises and invites
A nation e'en to join the jubilant strains,
Which celebrate thy consecrated days.[92]

SEEST THOU A MAN DILIGENT IN HIS BUSINESS? HE SHALL STAND
BEFORE KINGS; HE SHALL NOT STAND BEFORE MEAN MEN.

—PROVERBS 22:29

SHINING FOR JESUS

EFFIE WALLER SMITH

Brother, do you shine for Jesus,
Is your life a life of light;
Always radiant and brilliant,
Ever shining clear and bright?

Say, oh brother, are you shining,
Any time and anywhere,
Every day and every night,
Always shining bright and clear?

Do others see your light, dear brother,
And the good work that you do,
And are they constrained, dear brother,
To glorify your Father, too?

Does your blessed light, dear brother,
Ever grow the least bit dim,
Or your love and faith and patience,
Ever any less in Him?[93]

LET YOUR LIGHT SO SHINE BEFORE MEN, THAT THEY MAY SEE YOUR
GOOD WORKS, AND GLORIFY YOUR FATHER WHICH IS IN HEAVEN.

—MATTHEW 5:16

PHEBE ANN JACOBS

Phebe loved the Scriptures. Near by her, and always on her mind and heart, was her "precious Holy Bible," and her large-print Testament. Phebe had the same Bible that others have, but she found in it a great deal more than is commonly found, as all may observe who have seen her Bible. There the promises, and the threatenings and warnings too, are marked or underscored by her pen or pencil. Phebe's marks beneath or beside a passage, made often with a heavy stroke of her pencil, come to our minds with the force of a commentary, for she was herself a "living epistle," "known and read" by us all. Said her pastor, "If a thousand devoted Christians were requested to mark their favourite texts and expressions, it is believed they would hardly mark one not understood by Phebe."

Phebe loved the house of God. She took great delight in the services of the sanctuary: hence she was never absent except from sickness or urgent necessity. She was indeed a pillar of the church; one in whom the minister found support by her constant attendance and prayers, by her cordial reception and love of the truth. She was the first to be seated in her place at church. For many years, in our former house of worship, she was seen sitting in one corner of the gallery, on the furthest row of seats, with her head bowed in secret prayer. To look up to her as we entered the house of God was, to some of us at least, a prayer, a sermon, a hymn of praise. The last winter, her health failing, she was unable to walk to church as formerly and remained during the intermission—a season highly prized by some of her Christian friends, who would hasten back to meet her. That glowing look of hers, that close pressure of the hand, that Sabbath-day greeting, will never be forgotten. The best, the most experienced Christians, loved to be with Phebe because she was a happy, Bible Christian, a witness to the truth of God.

Phebe loved to pray. Many times a day would she go to her bedroom, carpeted as for a little sanctuary, and kneel and pray. So much was her soul awake to the interests of Zion, it was no uncommon occurrence for her to arise at midnight and pray. "At midnight I will arise, and give thanks unto Thee." This is a marked passage in her Bible. About four years since, her pastor was strengthened more than usual in his labors; his soul was richly fed with heavenly manna; and of this bread many of his flock partook with him. Not long after this season of refreshing, it was ascertained that Phebe had arisen every night, month after month, at midnight, to pray for her pastor.

Many were the individuals for whom she prayed. During the past winter a friend called to see her. "What is the good word?" said Phebe. "Anna is serious, and inquiring the way of life." She arose at once from her seat, lifted her hands, and with tears of joy praised God aloud, and said, "For her I have been praying; God is a hearer of prayer."

Phebe's faith and confidence in God were practical and availed her in time of need. When her mistress, Mrs. Allen, died, whom she loved more than any being on earth, and whose death was very sudden, in the dead of night, causing great distress in the family, Phebe calmly said, "Don't we pray, 'Thy will be done,' and now it is done?"

Phebe gave of her substance. She made a monthly contribution of fifty cents to missions, and bequeathed her little all, remaining after her decease, to the cause of Christ.

Phebe prayed for the college. The officers and students she bore on her heart to God. She always manifested a deep interest in the annual concert of prayer for colleges. At this concert, in the year 1834, a six o'clock morning prayer meeting was appointed. When the pastor came, he found that Phebe had been there on the doorsteps more than an hour praying! While it was yet dark, she found her way to the prayer meeting, as Mary to the sepulchre. Who can tell how many souls were converted in answer to the prayers on that doorstep—how much they had to do with those conversions in college which occurred at this time, and the fruits of which may be seen in the ministers scattered abroad, preaching the Gospel, gathering souls into the kingdom of Christ? Those seasons of revivals in college, have they no connection with the prayers of this humble saint, who lived to pray: lived in obscurity, and yet lived for the college; lived for the church; lived for the pastor; lived for the world?

. . . Phebe was humble. Her humility drew all hearts towards her. All the attention she received did not cause her for a moment to step aside from her own humble path, in which she continued to walk, doing her own work, or rather the Lord's, in her own humble, quiet way. She rarely, if ever, spoke first, yet was always ready to respond heartily to the greetings of her brethren and sisters in Christ. She literally and truly sought out the lowest seat. Down by the door at the evening meeting sat Phebe, with her head bowed, neither seeing nor wishing to be seen. Being urged to come up nearer, as she had often been before, it was said to her, "What will you do, Phebe, when you go to Heaven?" "My Master will tell me where to sit," she answered. There was a peculiar lowly attitude of spirit and manner which sat on her with a natural grace and beauty that cannot be described.

Phebe had no fear of death. She died as suddenly as her mistress, and now lies by her side in the Pinegrove cemetery, where lie so many of the loved and honoured. She had often expressed a desire to be placed at her mistress' feet. As she was expecting to die suddenly and alone, she had given the signal to her nearest neighbour, that when she saw no smoke from her chimney in the morning, she would know that she was gone. "When you hear I am gone home," said she to the writer of this, the Sabbath before she died, "praise the Lord. I shall go soon, very soon. If tomorrow you hear I am gone home to Heaven, rejoice and give thanks, and remember, it is well with me." "Jesus, lover of my soul," she repeated at this, our last Sabbath interview; "yes, lover, LOVER, LOVER! How can I better express it? 'Jesus, lover of my soul.'"[94]

WHAT IS THE EXCEEDING GREATNESS OF HIS POWER TO US-WARD WHO BELIEVE, ACCORDING TO THE WORKING OF HIS MIGHTY POWER, WHICH HE WROUGHT IN CHRIST, WHEN HE RAISED HIM FROM THE DEAD, AND SET HIM AT HIS OWN RIGHT HAND IN THE HEAVENLY PLACES, FAR ABOVE ALL PRINCIPALITY, AND POWER, AND MIGHT, AND DOMINION, AND EVERY NAME THAT IS NAMED, NOT ONLY IN THIS WORLD, BUT ALSO IN THAT WHICH IS TO COME.

—EPHESIANS 1:19-21

FREEDOM & FUTURE GLORY

IF THE SON THEREFORE SHALL MAKE YOU FREE,
YE SHALL BE FREE INDEED.

JOHN 8:36

For, you see, when all is said and done, freedom isn't that which you lose when someone fastens chains around your ankles and your wrists. It is that which you retain when you hold fast to those chains that bind you to the God of all. And that's a freedom that none can take away.

—Alan Keyes[95]

I want to influence my son's generation. I want to inspire my son's generation. I want to encourage my daughter's generation, but I'm not called to change their generation. I am called to change my generation. My contribution to their generation is the inspiration of watching me kill my giant and move this mountain, so that when they get up to the wheel they can say, "God, if you killed my daddy's giant, if you moved my daddy's mountain you can move mine."

—Bishop T. D. Jakes[96]

JOHN JASPER

Jasper's conviction as to his call to the ministry was clear-cut and intense. He believed that his call came straight from God. His boast and glory was that he was a God-made preacher. In his fierce warfares with the educated preachers of his race—"the new issue," as he contemptuously called them—he rested his claim on the ground that God had put him into the ministry; and so reverential, so full of noble assertion and so irresistibly eloquent was he in setting forth his ministerial authority, that even his most skeptical critics were constrained to admit that, like John the Baptist, he was "a man sent from God."

And yet Jasper knew the human side of his call. It was a part of his greatness that he could see truth in its relations and completeness, and while often he presented one side of a truth, as if it were all of it, he also saw the other side. With him a paradox was not a contradiction. He gratefully recognized the human influences which helped him to enter the ministry. While preaching one Sunday afternoon Jasper suddenly stopped, his face lighted as with a vision, a rich laugh rippled from his lips while his eyes flashed with soulful fire. He then said, in a manner never to be reported: "Mars Sam Hargrove called me to preach de Gospel—he was my old marster, and he started me out wid my message." Instantly the audience quivered with quickened attention, for they knew at once that the man in the pulpit had something great to tell.

"I was seeking God six long weeks . . .One July morning, something happened. I was stemming tobacco, and I took the tobacco leaf and tore the stem out, and no one at the factory could beat me at that work. But that morning, the stems wouldn't come out to save me, and I tore the tobacco by the pund, and flung it under the table. Actually, what was really going on was this: The darkness of death was in my soul that morning. My sins were piled on me like mountains; my feet were sinking down to the regions of despair, and I felt that of all sinners, I was the worst. I thought that I would die right then, an' with what I supposed was my last breath I flung up to Heaven a cry for mercy. Before I knew it, the light broke; I was light as a feather; my feet was on the mountain; salvation rolled like a flood through my soul, and I felt as if I could knock off the factory roof with my shouts!

"But I said to myself, I am going to hold still until dinner. And so, I cried and laughed, and tore up the tobacco. Then, I looked up at the table, and there was an old man—he loved me, but still, he tried hard to lead me out to the darkness. I whispered into his ear as low as I could, telling him, "Hallelujah, my soul is redeemed." Then, I jumped back into my work, but it was hard to keep my mouth shut. It wasn't long before I looked up, and there was a good old woman there who knew all my sorrows, and had been praying for me all the time. There was no use talking. I had to tell her. And I quietly skipped along near her and started to whisper in her ear about the goodness of the Lord. But what I thought would be a whisper was loud enough to be heard clear across James River to Manchester. One man said he thought the factory was falling down! All I know is this: I raised my first shout to the glory of my Redeemer.

"If it wasn't for a particular person, there would have been a genuine revival in the factory that morning. That particular person was the overseer. He burst into the room. And with a voice that sounded raspy, like he had flies for breakfast that morning, he bellowed out, 'What's all this about?' Somebody shouted that John Jasper got religion. But that didn't work with the boss. He told me to get back to my table, and he had something in his hand that looked ugly. It was no time for making fine points. So I said, 'Yes, sir, I meant no harm. The first taste of salvation got the better of me.'

"About that time, Mars Sam came out of his office and asked what was going on. The overseer told him. The devil told me to hate the overseer that morning, but the love of God was rolling through my soul, and somehow, I did not mind what he said.

"Soon after, I heard Mars Sam tell the overseer that he wanted to see Jasper. Mars Sam was a good man. He was a Baptist, and one of the head men of the First Baptist Church. I was glad to hear what he had to say to me. When I got to his office, he asked me what was going on out there. His voice was soft, as if it was a little song that played into my soul like an angel's harp. I said to him, 'Ever since the Fourth of July, I have been crying out to the Lord for six long weeks. Just now, I just realized that God had cleaned away all of my sins, and set my feet on a rock. I didn't mean to make any noise. But before I knew it, fire broke out in my soul, and I let out a shout to God my Savior.'

"Mars Sam was sitting with his eyes a little down to the floor, and with a quiver in his voice, he said very slowly, 'John, I believe that way myself. I love the Savior that you have just found, and I have no complaints that you made noise as you did.' Then, he did something that nearly made me drop to the floor. He got up from his chair, and walked over to me, and gave me his hand, saying, 'John, I wish you mighty well. Your Savior is mine. We are brothers in the Lord.' When he said that, I turned around and put my arm against the wall and held my mouth to keep from shouting. Mars Sam knew well the good he had done for me.

"After a while, he asked me, 'John, did you tell anyone out there about your conversion?' I said, 'Yes, before I knew it, I told them, and wanted to tell everyone in the whole world.' Then Mars Sam said, 'John, you may tell it. Go back in there, and go up and down the tables, and tell all of them. Then, go upstairs and tell them. Then, go downstairs and tell them. Then, go tell the hogshed men, and the drivers, and everyone, what the Lord has done for you.'

"By this time, Mars Sam's face was raining with tears. He told me, 'John, you don't need to work for me today. Take a holiday and go tell your neighbors, your family, and whoever you want, the good news. It'll do you good, do them good, and help to honor the Lord and Savior.'

"Oh that happy day! How can I ever forget it? That was my

conversion morning. That day, the Lord sent me out with the good news of the Kingdom. For more than forty years, I have been telling the story. My step is getting rather slow. My voice breaks down. And sometimes, I get awful tired. But I am still telling it. My lips shall proclaim the dying love of the Lamb with my last expiring breath.

"Ah, my dear old Master! He sleeps out in the cemetery, and in this world I shall see his face no more. But I will not forget him. He gave me a holiday to tell all my friends what the Lord had done for my soul. Often, as I preach, I feel that I am doing what my master told me to do. If he was here now, I think he would lift up them old black eyes of his, and say, 'That's right, John, still telling it. Fly like the angel, and wherever you go, carry the Gospel to the people.' Farewell old master, when I land in the heavenly city, I'll call your mansion that the Lord had made ready for you when you got there, and I will say, 'Mars Sam, I did what you told me, and many of them are coming up here with their robes washed in the blood of the Lamb, led into the Way by my preaching, and as you started me, I want you to share in the joy of their salvation.' And I reckon, when Mars Sam sees me, he will say, John, call me master no more. We are brothers now, and we will live together around the throne of God."

This is Jasper's story, but largely in his own broken words. When he told it, it swept over the great crowd like a celestial gale. The people seemed fascinated and transfigured. His homely way of putting the Gospel came home to them. Let me add that his allusions to his old master were in keeping with his kindly and conciliatory tone in all that he had to say about the white people after the emancipation of the slaves. He loved the white people, and among them his friends and lovers were counted by the thousand.[97]

JOHN JASPER'S PICTURE OF HEAVEN

WILLIAM E. HATCHER

I never heard Jasper preach a sermon on Heaven, nor did I ever hear of his doing so. So far as my observation goes, sermons on Heaven have failed to edify the thoughtful—sometimes proving distinctly disappointing. It was not to Jasper's taste to argue on Heaven as a doctrine. With him it was as if he were camping outside of a beautiful city, knowing much of its history and inhabitants, and in joyous expectation of soon moving into it.

The immediate things of the kingdom chiefly occupied his attention; but when his sermons took him into the neighborhood of Heaven, he took fire at once and the glory of the celestial city lit his face and cheered his soul. This chapter only deals with one of his sermons which, while not on Heaven, reveals his heart-belief in it and its vital effect upon his character.

Imagine a Sunday afternoon at his church—a fair, inspiring day. His house was thronged to overflowing. It was the funeral of two persons—William Ellyson and Mary Barnes. The text is forgotten, but the sermon is vividly recalled. From the start Jasper showed a burden and a boldness that promised rich things for his people. At the beginning he betrayed some hesitation—unusual for him.

"Let me say," he said, "a word about this William Ellyson. I'll say it first and get it off my mind. William Ellyson was no good man—he didn't say he was; he didn't try to be good, and they tell me he died as he lived—without God and hope in the world. It's a bad tale to tell on him, but he fixed the story himself. As the tree falls, there it must lay. If you want folks who live wrong to be preached and sung to glory, don't ask for Jasper. God comforts the mourner, and warns the unruly.

"But, my bretheren," he brightened as he spoke, "Mary Barnes was different. She was washed in the blood of the Lamb, and walked in the light. Her religion was of God. You could trust Mary anywhere. You'd never catch her in those playhouses, neither would you find her frisking in those dances. She was no streetwalker going round about. She loved the house of the Lord. Her feet clung to the straight and narrow path. I knew her well. I saw her at the prayer meeting, and at the supper, and I saw her while she was preaching. I saw her when she tended to the sick and helping the sinners who mourned. Our sister Mary, good-bye. Your race is run, but your crown is sure."

From this Jasper shot quite apart. He was full of fire, humour gleamed in his eye, and freedom was the bread of his soul. By degrees he approached the realm of death, and he went as an invader. A note of defiant challenge rang in his voice and almost blazed on his lips. He escorted the Christian to the court of death and demanded of the monster king to exhibit his power to hurt.

It was wonderful to see how he pictured the high courage of the child of God, marching up to the very face of the king of terrors and demanding that he come forth and do his worst. Death, on the other hand, was subdued, slow of speech, admitted his defeat, and proclaimed his readiness to serve the children of Immanuel. Then he affected to put his mouth to the grave and cried aloud:

"Grave! Grave! Oh Grave!" he cried as if addressing a real person, "where is your victory? I hear you got a mighty banner down there, an' you terrorize everyone that comes along this way. Bring out your armies and fly your banners of victory! Show me your hand, and let me see what you can do!" Then he made the grave reply: "I do not have victory. I had it, but Jesus passed through this country and tore down my banners. He says His people will not be troubled no more, forever! And He tells me that the gates are open, and let them pass on their way to glory."

"Oh, my God," Jasper exclaimed in a thrilling voice, "did you hear that? My Master Jesus jerked the sting of death, broke the scepter of the devil, and He went into the grave and robbed it of its victorious banners, and fixed a path, nice and smooth, for His people to pass through. Even more than that, He has written a song, a shouting anthem for us to sing when we go there, passing sun and stars, Thanks be unto God, who gives us the victory through the Lord Jesus Christ."

Too well I know that I do scant justice to the greatness of Jasper by this outline of his transcendent eloquence. The whole scene, distinct in every detail, was before the audience, and his responsive hearers were stirred into uncontrollable excitement.

"My brothers," Jasper resumed very soberly, "I often ask myself how I'd behave myself if I went to Heaven. I tell you I would tremble for the consequences. Even now, when I get a glimpse—just a peek—into the palace of the King, it overwhelms me to the point of awe and wonder. What will I do if I get there? I guess I'll make a fool of myself, because I don't exactly have the same nice manners and pretty ways my old master used to have. But if I get there, they ain't gonna put me out!

"First, I'll go to the river of life. Even here, I love to go down to the old muddy James River, which goes so grand and quiet, as if it was tending to business. But that is nothing compared to the river which flows by the throne. I long for its crystal waves, and the trees on the banks, and all manners of fruit. This old head of mine often gets hot with fever; I sometimes ache all night, and roll on the pillow. Many times, I have desired to cool it in the blessed stream as it kisses the banks of the upper Canaan. Blessed be the Lord! The thought of seeing that river, drinking its water, and resting under those trees. . ."

Then suddenly Jasper began to intone a chorus in a most affecting way, no part of which I can recall except the last line: "Oh, what must it be to be there?"

"After that," Jasper continued with quickened note, "I'd turn out and view the beauties of the city—the home of my Father. I'd stroll up those avenues where the children of God dwell and view their mansions. Father Abraham, I'm sure he has a great palace. And Moses, who escorted the children of Israel out of bondage through the wilderness and to the edge of the Promised Land, he must be powerfully set up, being such a rich man as he is. And David, the king that made the most beautiful songs. I'd like to see his home. And Paul, the mighty scholar who got struck down at Damascus' Road, I want to see his mansion."

As Jasper was moving at feeling pace along the path of his thoughts, he stopped and cried: "Look at that mighty sweet house, ain't it lovely?" Suddenly he sprang back and began to shout with joyous clapping of hands. "Look there; see that on the door! Hallelujah, it's John Jasper. Jesus said He was going to prepare a place for me; there it is! Too good for a poor sinner like me, but He built it for me, a turn-key job, and mine forever." Instantly he was singing his mellow chorus ending as before with: "Oh, what must it be to be there?"

From that scene, he moved off to see the angelic host. There were the white plains of the heavenly Canaan—a vast army of angels with their bands of music, their different ranks and grades, their worship before the throne and their pealing shouts as they broke around the throne of God. The charm of the scene was irresistible; it lifted everybody to a sight of Heaven, and it was all real to Jasper. He seemed entranced. As the picture began to fade, up rose his inimitable chorus, closing as always: "Oh, what must it be to be there?"

Then there was a long wait. But for the subdued and unworldly air of the old preacher—full seventy years old then—the delay
would have dissolved the spell. "And now friends," he said, still
panting and seeking to be calm, "if you'll excuse me, I'll take a trip
to the throne and see the King in His royal garments." It was an
event to study him at this point. His earnestness and reverence
passed all speech and grew as he went. The light from the throne
dazzled him from afar. There was the great white throne—there, the
elders bowing in adoring wonder—there, the archangels waiting in
silence for the commands of the King—there the King in His
resplendent glory—there in hosts innumerable were the ransomed.

In point of vivid description it surpassed all I had heard or
read. By this time the old Negro orator seemed glorified. Earth
could hardly hold him. He sprang about the platform with a boy's
alertness; he was unconsciously waving his handkerchief as if greeting a conqueror; his face was streaming with tears; he was bowing
before the Redeemer; he was clapping his hands, laughing, shouting, and wiping the blinding tears out of his eyes.

It was a moment of transport and unmatched wonder to everyone, and I felt as if it could never cease, when suddenly in a new
note he broke into his chorus, ending with the soul-melting words:
"Oh, what must it be to be there?"

It was a climax of climaxes. I supposed nothing else could
follow. We had been up so often and so high we could not be carried
up again. But there stood Jasper, fully seeing the situation. He had
seen it in advance and was ready.

"My brothers," said he as if in apology, "I forgot something. I
got to take another trip. I didn't visit the ransomed of the Lord. I
can't slight them. I know a heap of them, and I am bound to see
them." In a moment he had us out on the celestial plains with the

saints in line. There they were—countless and glorious!

We walked the whole line and had a sort of universal hand-shake in which no note of time was taken. "Here's brother Abel, the first man who got here. And brother Enoch, who took a stroll and walked right into glory. Here's old Elijah, who had a carriage sent for him, and came straightway into the city." Thus he went on greeting patriarchs, prophets, apostles, martyrs, his brethren and loved ones gone before until suddenly he sprang back and raised a shout that fairly shook the roof. As if by magic, things again changed and he was singing at the top of his voice the chorus which died away amid the shrieks and shouts of his crowd with his plaintive note: "Oh, what must it be to be there?"

Jasper dropped exhausted into a chair and some chief singer of the old-time sort, in noble scorn of all choirs, struck that wondrous old song, "When Death Shall Shake My Frame," and in a moment the great building throbbed and trembled with the mighty old melody. It was sung only as Jasper's race can sing, and especially as only Jasper's emotional and impassioned church could sing it.

This was Jasper's greatest sermon. In length it was not short of an hour and a half—maybe it was longer than that. He lifted things far above all thought of time, and not one sign of impatience was seen. The above sketch is all unworthy of the man or the sermon. As for the venerable old orator himself, he was in his loftiest mood—free in soul, alert as a boy, his imagination rioting, his action far outwent his words, and his pictures of celestial scenes glowed with unworldly luster. He was in Heaven that day, and took us around in his excursion wagon, and turning on the lights showed us the City of the Glorified.[98]

GOD SHALL WIPE AWAY ALL TEARS FROM THEIR EYES; AND THERE
SHALL BE NO MORE DEATH, NEITHER SORROW, NOR CRYING, NEI-
THER SHALL THERE BE ANY MORE PAIN: FOR THE FORMER THINGS
ARE PASSED AWAY.

—REVELATION 21:4

JOSIAH HENSON

*The numerous friends of the author of this little work
will need no greater recommendation than his name to
make it welcome. Among all the singular and interesting
records to which the institution of American slavery has
given rise, we know of none more striking, more charac-
teristic and instructive, than that of Josiah Henson.*

*Born a slave—a slave in effect in a heathen land—and
under a heathen master, he grew up without Christian
light or knowledge, and like the Gentiles spoken of by St.
Paul, "without the law did by nature the things that are
written in the law." One sermon, one offer of salvation by
Christ, was sufficient for him, as for the Ethiopian
eunuch, to make him at once a believer from the heart
and a preacher of Jesus.*

*To the great Christian doctrine of forgiveness of enemies
and the returning of good for evil, he was by God's grace
made a faithful witness, under circumstances that try
men's souls and make us all who read it say, "lead us not
into such temptation." We earnestly commend this portion of his narrative to those who, under much smaller*

temptations, think themselves entitled to render evil for evil.

The African race appear as yet to have been companions only of the sufferings of Christ. In the melancholy scene of His death—while Europe in the person of the Roman delivered him unto death, and Asia in the person of the Jew clamored for His execution—Africa was represented in the person of Simon the Cyrenean, who came patiently bearing after Him the load of the Cross; and ever since then poor Africa has been toiling on, bearing the weary cross of contempt and oppression after Jesus.

But they who suffer with Him shall also reign; and when the unwritten annals of slavery shall appear in the judgment, many Simons who have gone meekly bearing their cross after Jesus to unknown graves, shall rise to thrones and crowns! Verily a day shall come when He shall appear for these His hidden ones, and then "many that are last shall be first, and the first shall be last."

—HARRIET BEECHER STOWE

TRUTH STRANGER THAN FICTION

My heart exults with gratitude when I mention the name of a good man who first taught me the blessedness of religion. His name was John McKenny. He lived at Georgetown, a few miles only from Riley's plantation; his business was that of a baker, and his character was that of an upright, benevolent Christian.

He was noted especially for his detestation of slavery and his resolute avoidance of the employment of slave labor in his business. He would not even hire a slave, the price of whose toil must be paid to his master, but contented himself with the work of his own hands, and with such free labor as he could procure. His reputation was high, not only for this almost singular abstinence from what no one about him thought wrong, but for his general probity and excellence. This man occasionally served as a minister of the Gospel, and preached in a neighborhood where preachers were somewhat rare at that period.

One Sunday when he was to officiate in this way, at a place three or four miles distant, my mother urged me to ask master's permission to go and hear him. I had so often been beaten for making such a request that I refused to make it. She still persisted, telling me that I could never become a Christian if I minded beatings— that I must take up my cross and bear it. She was so grieved at my refusal that she wept. To gratify her I concluded to try the experiment, and accordingly went to my master and asked permission to attend the meeting.

Although such permission was not given freely or often, yet his favor to me was shown for this once by allowing me to go, without much scolding, but not without a pretty distinct intimation of what would befall me if I did not return immediately after the close of the service. I hurried off, pleased with the opportunity, but without any definite expectations of benefit or amusement; for up to this period of my life, and I was then eighteen years old, I had never heard a sermon, nor any discourse or conversation whatever, upon religious topics, except what I had heard from my mother on the responsibility of all to a Supreme Being. When I arrived at the place of meeting, the services were so far advanced that the speaker was just beginning his discourse, from the text, Hebrews 2:9: "That he

by the grace of God should taste of death for every man." This was
the first text of the Bible to which I had ever listened, knowing it to
be such. I have never forgotten it, and scarcely a day has passed
since, in which I have not recalled it and the sermon that was
preached from it.

The divine character of Jesus Christ, His tender love for
mankind, His forgiving spirit, His compassion for the outcast and
despised, His cruel crucifixion and glorious ascension, were all
depicted, and some of the points were dwelt on with great power;
great, at least, to me, who then heard of these things for the first
time in my life.

Again and again did the preacher reiterate the words "for every
man." These glad tidings, this salvation, were not for the benefit of
a select few only. They were for the slave as well as the master, the
poor as well as the rich, for the persecuted, the distressed, the
heavy-laden, the captive; for me among the rest, a poor, despised,
abused creature, deemed of others fit for nothing but unrequited
toil—but mental and bodily degradation.

O, the blessedness and sweetness of feeling that I was LOVED!
I would have died that moment, with joy, for the compassionate
Saviour about whom I was hearing. "He loves me," "He looks down
in compassion from heaven on me," "He died to save my soul,"
"He'll welcome me to the skies," I kept repeating to myself. I was
transported with delicious joy. I seemed to see a glorious being, in a
cloud of splendor, smiling down from on high.

In sharp contrast with the experience of the contempt and bru-
tality of my earthly master, I basked in the sunshine of the benigni-
ty of this divine being. "He'll be my dear refuge—He'll wipe away
all tears from my eyes." "Now I can bear all things; nothing will
seem hard after this." I felt sorry that "Massa Riley" didn't know
Him, sorry he should live such a coarse, wicked, cruel life.
Swallowed up in the beauty of the divine love, I loved my enemies,

and prayed for them that did despitefully use and entreat me.

Revolving the things which I had heard in my mind as I went home, I became so excited that I turned aside from the road into the woods and prayed to God for light and for aid with an earnestness, which, however unenlightened, was at least sincere and heartfelt; and which the subsequent course of my life has led me to imagine was acceptable to Him who heareth prayer. At all events, I date my conversion, and my awakening to a new life—a consciousness of power and a destiny superior to anything I had before conceived of—from this day, so memorable to me.

I used every means and opportunity of inquiry into religious matters; and so deep was my conviction of their superior importance to everything else, so clear my perception of my own faults, and so undoubting my observation of the darkness and sin that surrounded me, that I could not help talking much on these subjects with those about me; and it was not long before I began to pray with them, and exhort them, and to impart to the poor slaves those little glimmerings of light from another world, which had reached my own eye. In a few years I became quite an esteemed preacher among them, and I will not believe it is vanity which leads me to think I was useful to some.[99]

BUT BY THE GRACE OF GOD I AM WHAT I AM: AND HIS GRACE
WHICH WAS BESTOWED UPON ME WAS NOT IN VAIN; BUT I
LABOURED MORE ABUNDANTLY THAN THEY ALL: YET NOT I, BUT
THE GRACE OF GOD WHICH WAS WITH ME.

—1 CORINTHIANS 15:10

INDEX OF NAMES

John Quincy Adams (97, 98, 125)

Thomas Anderson (86)

Maya Angelou (146)

Wellington Boone (79, 160)

V. W. Broughton (130)

Henry "box" Brown (36)

Les Brown (103, 162)

George Washington Carver (120)

John Henrik Clarke (62)

Andrae Crouch (146)

Gail Devers (32)

Frederick Douglass (141)

W.E.B. DuBois (62)

Old Elizabeth (111)

Anthony Evans (40, 124)

Julia A. J. Foote (126)

Al Green (79)

A.V. Griswold (115)

Fred Hammond (67)

Josephine Delphine Henderson Heard (41, 99, 101)

Josiah Henson (183)

Howard Hewitt (40)

Evander Holyfield (38)

George M. Horton (68)

Bo Jackson (105)

Mahalia Jackson (66)

Phebe Ann Jacobs (166)

T.D. Jakes (103, 171)

John Jasper (171, 176)

John Jea (88)

Thomas L. Johnson (135, 137)

Alan Keyes (105, 159, 171)

Dr. Martin Luther King Jr. (63, 70, 83)

Lucy Larcom (119)

Jarena Lee (50)

Carl Lewis (79)

Nelson Mandela (64)

Mary F. McCray (156)

Joanna P. Moore (120)

Otis Moss (124)

Jesse Owens (160)

Rosa Parks (64)

Ann Plato (43)

Peter Randolf (133)

H. Cordelia Ray (150, 164)

Condoleezza Rice (40, 62, 105, 147)

David Robinson (160)

Jackie Robinson (38, 79)

Barry Sanders (161)

Effie Waller Smith (73, 74, 110, 128, 165)

Maria Stewart (70)

Harriett Beecher Stowe (182)

Clara Ann Thompson (48, 49, 75, 108, 147)

Theodore Tilton (155)

Charles Tindley (46, 76, 106, 163)

Sojourner Truth (52, 77, 80, 90, 96)

Harriett Tubman (85, 86)

Desmond Tutu (63, 103)

Cicely Tyson (32)

Herschel Walker (105)

Booker T. Washington (6, 64)

J.C. Watts (160, 161)

Phyllis Wheatley (32, 34, 53, 56, 57, 95, 106)

ENDNOTES

1. The Nobel Foundation.

2. Ibid.

3. http://www.gaildevers.com/biography.htm.

4. Judy Klimeesrud, "Cicely, the Looker from Sounder."

5. Phyllis Wheatley, *Poems on Various Subjects, Religious and Moral,* Printed for A. Bell, Bookseller, Aldgate and sold by Messrs. Cox and Berry, King Street, Boston, 1773.

6. Ibid.

7. G. W. Offley, *A Narrative of the Life and Labors of the Rev. G. W. Offley, a Colored Man, Local Preacher and Missionary; Who Lived Twenty-Seven Years at the South and Twenty-Three at the North; Who Never Went to School a Day in His Life, and Only Commenced to Learn His Letters When Nineteen Years and Eight Months Old; the Emancipation of His Mother and Her Three Children; How He Learned to Read While Living in a Slave State, and Supported Himself from the Time He Was Nine Years Old Until He Was Twenty-One,* Washington: Greensbury.

8. Henry Brown, *Narrative of the Life of Henry "box" Brown, Written by Himself,* Manchester: Printed by Lee and Glynn, 1851.

9. *Christianity Today,* March/April, 1998

10. Richard Newman, *African-American Quotations,* Onyx Press, 1998.

11. Tony Evans, *Totally Saved,* Moody Publishers, 2002.

12. Howard Hewitt, Interview with GospelFlava.com, *Ministering Beyond Boundaries.*

13. *Biography* Magazine, September 2001.

14. Josephine Delphine Henderson Heard, *Morning Glories,* Philadelphia, 1890.

15. Ann Plato, *Essays Including Biographies and Miscellaneous Pieces, in Prose and Poetry,* Hartford, 1841.

16. Charles Tindley, *Beams of Heaven (Someday).*

17. Clara Ann Thompson, *Songs from the Wayside, Published and Sold by the Author,* Ohio: Rossmoyne, 1908.

18. Ibid.

19. Jarena Lee, *Religious Experience and Journal of Mrs. Jarena Lee, Giving an Account of Her Call to Preach the Gospel, Revised and Corrected from the Original Manuscript, Written by Herself.*

20. Phyllis Wheatley, *Poems on Various Subjects, Religious and Moral,* Printed for A. Bell, Bookseller, Aldgate and sold by Messrs. Cox and Berry, King Street, Boston, 1773.

21. Ibid.

22. *Biography* Magazine, September 2001.

23. Richard Newman, *African-American Quotations,* Onyx Press, 1998.

24. Ibid.

25. Ibid.

26. Nobel Prize Acceptance Speech, 1984, Oslo, Norway.
http://www.dadalos.org/int/Vorbilder/Vorbilder/tutu/nobelpreis.htm

27. Nobel Prize acceptance speech, 1993.

28. Speech in Atlanta, September 18, 1895.

29. Rosa Parks on the occasion of her 77th birthday.

30. Mahalia Jackson, *How I Got Over*.

31. Fred Hammond, Lyrics from *When Love Calls You Home, Matters of the Heart*, 1994.

32. George Moses Horton, *The Poetical Works of George M. Horton, The Colored Bard of North Carolina, To Which Is Prefixed the Life of the Author, Written by Himself*, 1880.

33. Maria Stewart, Farewell Address in New York, April 14, 1834.

34. Effie Waller Smith, *Songs of the Months*, New York: Broadway Publishing Company, 1904.

35. Ibid.

36. Clara Ann Thompson, *Songs from the Wayside*, Rossmoyne, Ohio, 1908.

37. Hymn: Words and Music by Charles A. Tindley, 1916.

38. Sojourner Truth, Olive Gilbert, and Frances W. Titus, *Narrative of Sojourner Truth; a Bondswoman of Olden Time, Emancipated by the New York Legislature in the Early Part of the Present Century; with a History of Her Labors and Correspondence.*

39. *Sepia* Magazine, March 1973.

40. http://www.africanamericans.com/JackieRobinson.htm

41. http://www.topendsports.com/psychology/quotes-motivate.htm

42. Olive Gilbert and Sojourner Truth, *Narrative of Sojourner Truth, a Northern Slave, Emancipated from Bodily Servitude by the State of New York*, 1828.

43. Martin Luther King Jr., *A Letter from a Birmingham, Alabama, Jail*, April 16th, 1963.

44. Sarah H. Bradford, *Harriet: The Moses of Her People*, New York: George R. Lockwood & Son, 1886.

45. Thomas Anderson, *Interesting Account of Thomas Anderson, a Slave, Taken from His Own Lips.*

46. John Jea, *The Life, History, and Unparalleled Sufferings of John Jea, the African Preacher*, Compiled and Written by Himself.

47. Olive Gilbert and Sojourner Truth, *Narrative of Sojourner Truth, a Northern Slave, Emancipated from Bodily Servitude by the State of New York*, 1828.

48. Phyllis Wheatley, *Poems on Various Subjects, Religious and Moral*, Printed for A. Bell, Bookseller, Aldgate and sold by Messrs. Cox and Berry, King Street, Boston, 1773.

49. Olive Gilbert and Sojourner Truth, *Narrative of Sojourner Truth, a Northern Slave, Emancipated from Bodily Servitude by the State of New York*, 1828, p. 312.

50. *Narrative of the Life of John Quincy Adams, When in Slavery, and Now as a Freeman*, Pennsylvania: Harrisburg, 1872.

51. Ibid.

52. Josephine Delphine Henderson Heard, *Morning Glories*, Philadelphia, 1890.

53. Ibid.

54. Les Brown, *Live Your Dreams*, Perennial Currents, 1994.

55. Response by Archbishop Tutu on his appointment as Chairperson of the Truth and Reconciliation Commission, November 30, 1995.

56. *Maximizing Moments*, Beliefnet.com, http://www.beliefnet.com/story/83/story_8361_2.html

57. Black Americans for Life Banquet, Adam's Mark Hotel, Indianapolis, Indiana, November 4, 1995.

58. http://www.imdb.com/name/nm1110666/bio

59. http://www.topendsports.com/psychology/quotes-motivate.htm

60. http://www.topendsports.com/psychology/quotes-motivate.htm

61. Phyllis Wheatley, *Poems on Various Subjects, Religious and Moral*, Printed for A. Bell, Bookseller, Aldgate and sold by Messrs. Cox and Berry, King Street, Boston, 1773.

62. Hymn: Words and Music by Charles A. Tindley, 1905.

63. Clara Ann Thompson, *Songs from the Wayside*, Rossmoyne, Ohio, 1900.

64. Effie Waller Smith, *Songs of the Months*, New York: Broadway Publishing Company, 1904.

65. *Memoir of Old Elizabeth, A Coloured Woman*, Philadelphia: Collins, 1863.

66. *A Narrative of Griswold, the African Youth, From the Mission School at Cape Palmas, Who Died in Boston May 16, 1844*, Boston: Published by a Friend of Missions, 1845.

67. Joanna P. Moore, *"In Christ's Stead": Autobiographical Sketches*.

68. Tony Evans, *Totally Saved*, Moody Publishers, 2002.

69. Ibid.

70. Richard Newman, *African-American Quotations*, Onyx Press, 1998.

71. *Narrative of the Life of John Quincy Adams, When in Slavery, and Now as a Freeman*, Pennsylvania: Harrisburg, 1872.

72. Ibid.

73. Julia A. J. Foote, *A Brand Plucked from the Fire: An Autobiographical Sketch by Mrs. Julia A. J. Foote*.

74. Effie Waller Smith, *Songs of the Months*, New York: Broadway Publishing Company, 1904.

75. Virginia Broughton, *Twenty Years' Experience of a Missionary*, Chicago: W Pony Press, 1907.

76. Peter Randolph, *Sketches of Slave Life or Illustrations of the "Peculiar Institution."*

77. Ed Stroud Smith.

78. Thomas Lewis Johnson, *Twenty-Eight Years a Slave or the Story of My Life in Three Continents.*

79. Frederick Douglass, *Life and Times of Frederick Douglass, Written by Himself.*

80. Interview with *Gospel Flava*.

http://www.gospelflava.com/articles/andraecrouchinterview1.html

81. *Biography* Magazine, September 2001.

82. Clara Ann Thompson, *Songs from the Wayside*, Rossmoyne, Ohio, 1900.

83. H. Cordelia Ray, *Poems by H. Cordelia Ray*, New York: The Grafton Press, 1910.

84. Charles Waddell Chesnutt, *Frederick Douglass: 1858-1932*, Ed. By M. A. De Wolfe Howe.

85. *Life of Mary F. McCray, Born and Raised a Slave in the State of Kentucky by Her Husband and Son*, Lima, Ohio, 1898.

86. http://www.jesseowens.com/quote2.html.

87. National Recreation and Park Association, Gale Group, 2003, http://www.find-articles.com/p/articles/mi_m1145/is_7_38/ai_106226899.

88. Wayne Drehs, "Happy Sanders Shows Crowd Different Side," http://espn.go.com/classic/s/2004/0808/1855156.html.

89. House Conference Chairman J.C. Watts, Jr., Keynote Address, National Rifle Association Annual Convention, Charlotte, N.C, 2000.

90. Les Brown, *Live Your Dreams*, Perennial Currents, 1994.

91. Hymn: Words and Music by Charles A. Tindley, 1905.

92. H. Cordelia Ray, *Poems by H. Cordelia Ray*, New York: The Grafton Press, 1910.

93. Effie Waller Smith, *Songs of the Months*, New York: Broadway Publishing Company, 1904.

94. Mrs. T. C. Upham, *Narrative of Phebe Ann Jacobs*, W. and F. G. Cash, 1850.

95. Black Americans for Life Banquet, Adam's Mark Hotel, Indianapolis, Indiana, November 4, 1995.

96. Bishop T. D. Jakes, Sermon: "All I Have Is A Seed On My Side."

97. William Eldridge Hatcher, *John Jasper: The Unmatched Negro Philosopher and Preacher.*

98. Ibid.

99. Josiah Henson, *Truth Stranger Than Fiction: Father Henson's Story of His Own Life.*

Additional copies of this book and other titles from Honor Books
are available from your local bookstore.

The following titles are also available
in the African American Heritage Series:

God Has Soul:

Celebrating the Indomitable Spirit of African Americans

Soul Cry:

Powerful Prayers from the Spiritual Heritage of African Americans

Soul Praise:

*Amazing Stories Behind the Great African-American Hymns
and Negro Spirituals*

If you have enjoyed this book,
or if it has impacted your life,
we would like to hear from you.

Please contact us at:
Honor Books,
An imprint of Cook Communications Ministries
4050 Lee Vance View
Colorado Springs, CO 80918